U0799574

Overview of Traditional Chinese Culture

中国传统文化概览

主　编　王　翠
副主编　张锦辉

Beijing
Metallurgical Industry Press
2023

Metallurgical Industry Press
39 Songzhuyuan North Alley, Dongcheng District, Beijing 100009, China

Copyright © Metallurgical Industry Press 2023. All rights reserved.

No part of this publication may be reproduced or transmitted in any form or by any means, electronic or mechanical, including photocopying, recording, or any information storage and retrieval system, without permission in writing from the copyright owner.

图书在版编目(CIP)数据

中国传统文化概览=Overview of Traditional Chinese Culture：英文/王翠主编.—北京：冶金工业出版社，2023.5

ISBN 978-7-5024-8668-6

Ⅰ.①中…　Ⅱ.①王…　Ⅲ.①中华文化—概论—英文　Ⅳ.①K203

中国版本图书馆 CIP 数据核字(2020)第 261803 号

Overview of Traditional Chinese Culture

出版发行 冶金工业出版社		**电　话** (010)64027926	
地　址 北京市东城区嵩祝院北巷 39 号		**邮　编** 100009	
网　址 www.mip1953.com		**电子信箱** service@mip1953.com	

责任编辑　张熙莹　郭雅欣　美术编辑　郑小利　版式设计　孙跃红
责任校对　郑　娟　责任印制　禹　蕊
北京建宏印刷有限公司印刷
2023 年 5 月第 1 版，2023 年 5 月第 1 次印刷
710mm×1000mm　1/16；8 印张；156 千字；120 页
定价 36.00 元

投稿电话　(010)64027932　投稿信箱　tougao@cnmip.com.cn
营销中心电话　(010)64044283
冶金工业出版社天猫旗舰店　yjgycbs.tmall.com
(本书如有印装质量问题，本社营销中心负责退换)

本书编委会

主　编　王　翠

副主编　张锦辉

编　委　吴颖芳　刘　晓　李　燕　陈　阳
　　　　　李　莉　王立秀

Preface

The Chinese traditional culture has a long history. President Xi Jinping points out, "We have the confidence and necessity to tell China's story." "Storytelling is the best form of international communication." "We need to make great efforts to enhance our international communication capacity." With its five thousand years of history, the Chinese nation attracts attention with unique inventions in the world. China's unique philosophy, delicacies, curls of fragrant tea, architectural gardens, poetry and literature, comedy and opera, traditional Chinese medicine and holiday, all reflect the unparalleled wisdom of the Chinese people in the construction of their homes and the long-term labor of national development. These eventually become the spiritual source and cultural genes of the Chinese nation. In order to respond to the trend of national rejuvenation, increase the publicity of China to the world, and make a strong voice of China, I edit this book specially.

This book is written with the following four outstanding features: firstly, introducing Chinese cultural characteristics in authentic and fluent English, suitable for college students and other readers of different levels to read and learn English; secondly, the selected content of Chinese characteristics pays attention to interesting reading, so readers of different levels will have a strong interest in reading, to obtain a pleasant reading experience; thirdly, the amount of information on the same topic is appropriate, so that readers can easily construct the knowledge system of the subject when they come into contact with a cultural theme, and also improve their English reading and strengthen their language knowledge acquisition; Fourthly, after each cultural theme article, the book is accompanied by rich forms of exercises for students and other readers to refer to, review and consolidate the content of the article and language knowledge.

The compilation of this book requires the collection of a large number of

English materials and articles, and the editing work is very complicated. Here, the editor will send sincere thanks to all the leaders and editorial committee who participated in the preparation of the book. Thanks to Dean Ma Yingxin and Vice Premier Zhang Jinhui for their guidance.

Due to the limited level of writing, experience needs to be improved, this book inevitably occurs mistakes and omissions, welcome readers to criticize and correct all shortcoming.

Cui Wang

2022. 10

Contents

Unit 1 Chinese Philosophy

The favorable opportunity does not help as much as the favorable terrain; the favorable terrain does not help as much as the group morale.

——Mencius

Unit Goals

- To get familiar with the development of Chinese philosophy.
- To get familiar with the five main schools of Chinese philosophy and their ideas.
- To learn about the similarities and differences between Chinese and western philosophies.
- To learn useful words and expressions concerning philosophical concepts and improve English language skills.

Before You Read

1. Give the names of the following philosophers according to the pictures.

2. Look at the pictures above and then discuss the following questions with your partners.

(1) Tell the origin of Chinese philosophy briefly.

(2) Name a few well-known Chinese philosophers and share one story with your partner.

Intensive Reading

Text A
History of Chinese Philosophy

It is known that early Shang Dynasty (1600 BC - 1046 BC) thought was based on cyclicity, from observation of the cycles of day and night, the seasons, the moon, etc., a concept which remained relevant throughout later Chinese philosophy, and immediately setting it apart from the more linear Western approach. During this time, both gods and ancestors were worshipped and there were human and animal sacrifices.

During the succeeding Zhou Dynasty (1122 BC—256 BC), the concept of the Mandate of Heaven was introduced, which held that Heaven would bless the authority of a just ruler, but would be displeased with an unwise ruler, and retract the Mandate.

The "*Classic of Changes*" was traditionally compiled by the mythical figure Fu Xi in the 28th century BC, although modern research suggests that it more likely dates to the late 9th century BC. The text describes an ancient system of cosmology and philosophy that is intrinsic to ancient Chinese cultural beliefs, centering on the ideas of the dynamic balance of opposites, the evolution of events as a process, and acceptance of the inevitability of change. It consists of a series of symbols, rules for manipulating these symbols, poems and commentary, and is sometimes regarded as a system of divination.

In about 500 BC, the classic period of Chinese philosophy——known as the Contention of a Hundred Schools of Thought——flourished, and the four most influential schools (Confucianism, Taoism, Mohism and Legalism) were established.

During the Qin Dynasty (also known as the Imperial Era), after the unification of China in 221 BC, Legalism became ascendant at the expense of the Mohist and Confucianist schools, although the Han Dynasty (206 BC - 220 AD) adopted Taoism and later Confucianism as official doctrine. Along with the gradual parallel introduction of Buddhism, these two schools have remained the determining forces of Chinese thought up until the 20th century.

Neo-Confucianism (a variant of Confucianism, incorporating elements of Buddhism, Taoism and Legalism) was introduced during the Song Dynasty (960 AD-1279) and popularized during the Ming Dynasty (1368-1644).

During the Industrial and Modern Ages, Chinese philosophy also began to integrate concepts of western philosophy. Sun Yat-sen (1866-1925) attempted to incorporate elements of democracy, republicanism and industrialism at the beginning of the 20th century, while Mao Zedong (1893-1976) later added Marxism, Stalinism and other communist thought. During the Cultural Revolution of 1966-1976, most previous schools of thought, with the notable exception of Legalism, were denounced as backward and purged, although their influence has remained.

Vocabulary

ancestor *n.* 始祖，祖先；被继承人
retract *vt.* 缩回；缩进；取消
intrinsic *adj.* 本质的，固有的
manipulate *v.* 操纵
ascendant *n.* 优势
succeeding *adj.* 随后的，接着的
cosmology *n.* ［天］宇宙论，［天］宇宙学
dynamic *adj.* 动态的
divination *n.* 预测，占卜
doctrine *n.* 教条，主义

After You Read

Exercises

1. Answer the following questions.

(1) What is the philosophical thought of Shang Dynasty?
(2) What is the philosophical thought of Zhou Dynasty?
(3) What is the main idea of the "*Classic of Changes*"?
(4) What is the primary school of philosophy of Qin Dynasty?
(5) What are the philosophical schools remain influential in modern China?

2. Fill in the blanks with the words given below. Change the form where necessary. Each word can be used only once.

authority	inevitability	manipulate	divination	contention
unification	incorporate	popularize	integrate	denounce

(1) With the development of society, piano use of the teaching ________ more

and more in music.

(2) If the case succeeds, it is ____________ that other trials will follow.

(3) The International Red Cross Movement grew out of a major battle in the ______ ______ of Italy.

(4) These compasses were south pointing and were primarily used on land as ______ ______ tools and direct finders.

(5) She's always borrowing my clothes and ____________ me to give her vast sums of money.

(6) This provided a pretext for the ____________ to cancel the elections.

(7) It is my ____________ that death and murder always lurk as potentials in violent relationships.

(8) The agreement would allow the rebels to be ____________ into a new national police force.

(9) Some ____________ it for doing less to curb greenhouse gases than was once promised.

(10) He thinks we are living in a fully ____________, supportive society.

3. Decide whether the statements are true (T) or false (F) according to the passage.

(1) The western approach of philosophy is linear, while the Chinese approach is circular.

(2) The ideas of the dynamic balance of opposites, the evolution of events as a process, and authority of a just ruler are all from the "*Classic of Changes*".

(3) The four most influential schools (Confucianism, Taoism, Mohism and Legalism) were established after Qin Dynasty.

(4) Confucianism popularized during the Ming Dynasty.

(5) Legalism is the only philosophical school preserved in modern China.

4. Translation

(1) It is known that early Shang Dynasty (1600 BC–1046 BC) thought was based on cyclicity, from observation of the cycles of day and night, the seasons, the moon, etc., a concept which remained relevant throughout later Chinese philosophy, and immediately setting it apart from the more linear Western approach.

(2) During the succeeding Zhou Dynasty (1122 BC–256 BC), the concept of the

Mandate of Heaven was introduced, which held that Heaven would bless the authority of a just ruler, but would be displeased with an unwise ruler, and retract the Mandate.

(3) The text describes an ancient system of cosmology and philosophy that is intrinsic to ancient Chinese cultural beliefs, centering on the ideas of the dynamic balance of opposites, the evolution of events as a process, and acceptance of the inevitability of change.

(4) In about 500 BC, the classic period of Chinese philosophy——known as the Contention of a Hundred Schools of Thought——flourished, and the four most influential schools (Confucianism, Taoism, Mohism and Legalism) were established.

(5) During the Qin Dynasty (also known as the Imperial Era), after the unification of China in 221 BC, Legalism became ascendant at the expense of the Mohist and Confucianist schools, although the Han Dynasty (206 BC - 220 AD) adopted Taoism and later Confucianism as official doctrine.

5. Pair work

Read a well-known philosopher and tell your partner about the story in English. And then share the best story and comments in class.

Read More

Extensive Reading

Text B
The Main Schools of Chinese Philosophy

Confucianism

This school was developed from the teachings of the sage Confucius (551 BC-479 BC), and collected in the *Analects of Confucius*. It is a system of moral, social, political, and quasi-religious thought, whose influence also spreads to Korea and Japan. The major Confucian concepts include *Ren* (humanity or humaneness), *Tianming* (similar to the concept of the mandate of Heaven), *Zhong* (loyalty), *Xiao* (filial piety), and *Li* (ritual). It introduced the Golden Rule (essentially, treat others as you would like to be treated), the concept of *Yin* and *Yang* (two opposing forces that are permanently in conflict with each other, leading to perpetual contradiction and change), the idea of meritocracy, and of reconciling opposites in order to arrive at some middle ground combining the best of both. Confucianism is not necessarily regarded as a religion, allowing one to be a Taoist, Christian, Muslim, Shintoist or Buddhist and still profess Confucianist beliefs. Arguably the most famous Confucian after Confucius himself was Meng Tzu (or Mencius) (372 BC-289 BC)

Taoism

Sometimes also written Daoism, Taoism is a philosophy which later also developed into a religion. Tao literally means "path" or "way", although it is more often used as a meta-physical term that describes the flow of the universe, or the force behind the natural order. The Three Jewels of the Tao are compassion, moderation, and humility. Taoist thought focuses on *Wuwei* ("non-action"), spontaneity, humanism, relativism, emptiness and the strength of softness (or flexibility). Nature and ancestor spirits are common in popular Taoism, although typically there is also a pantheon of gods, often headed by the Jade Emperor. The most influential Taoist text is the "*Tao Te Ching*" (or "*Daodejing*") written around the 6th Century BC by Lao Tzu (or Laozi), and a secondary text is the 4th century BC "*Zhuangzi*", named after its author. The *Yin* and *Yang* symbol is important in Taoist symbology (as in Confucianism), as are the Eight Trigrams, and a zigzag with seven stars which represent the Big Dipper star constellation.

Legalism

Legalism is a pragmatic political philosophy, whose main motto is "set clear strict laws, or deliver harsh punishment", and its essential principle is one of jurisprudence. According to Legalism, a ruler should govern his subjects according to *Fa* (law or principle), *Shu* (method, tactic, art, or statecraft) and *Shi* (legitimacy, power, or charisma). Under Li Si in the 3rd century BC, a form of Legalism essentially became a totalitarian ideology in China, which in part led to its subsequent decline.

Buddhism

Buddhism is a religion, a practical philosophy and arguably a psychology, focusing on the teachings of Buddha (Siddhartha Gautama), who lived in India from the mid-6th to the early 5th century BC. It was introduced to China from India, probably some time during the 1st century BC. Chinese tradition focuses on ethics rather than metaphysics, and it developed several schools distinct from the originating Indian schools, and in the process integrated the ideas of Confucianism, Taoism and other indigenous philosophical systems into itself. The most prominent Chinese Buddhist school sare *Sanlun*, *Tiantai*,

Huayan and *Chán* (known as *Zen* in Japan).

Mohism

Mohism was founded by Mozi (c. 470 BC–390 BC). It promotes universal love with the aim of mutual benefit, such that everyone must love each other equally and impartially to avoid conflict and war. Mozi was strongly against Confucian ritual, instead emphasizing pragmatic survival through farming, fortification and statecraft. In some ways, his philosophy parallels Western utilitarianism. Although popular during the latter part of the Zhou Dynasty, many Mohist texts were destroyed during the succeeding Qin Dynasty, and it was finally supplanted completely by Confucianism during the Han Dynasty.

Vocabulary

perpetual *adj.* 永恒的
compassion *n.* 同情
jurisprudence *n.* 法学 [正式]
indigenous *adj.* 本土的；当地的 [正式]
utilitarianism *n.* 功利主义 [技术]
meritocracy *n.* 贤能社会
pragmatic *adj.* 务实的
metaphysics *n.* 玄学；形而上学
fortification *n.* 防御工事
supplant *vt.* 取代 [正式]

Exercises

1. Global reading

Decide whether the following statements are true (T) or false (F).

(1) In Confucius's ideas, *ren* is the general principle while virtue is the guiding line of conduct.

(2) "*Wuwei*" in Taoism recommended a policy of doing nothing and just accepting what happens to one.

(3) The "harsh punishment" motto of Legalism definitely led to its decline.

(4) Buddhism is an integration of the ideas of Indian Buddhism, Confucianism, Taoism and other indigenous philosophical systems.

(5) The ideas of Mohism is completely opposite to those of Confucianism.

2. Questions for discussion

(1) What are the main thoughts of Confucianism?

(2) What does Taoist thought mainly focus on?

(3) What are the similarities and differences between Confucianism and Mohism?

3. Classroom activities

(1) Can you give a brief account of the philosophies of Confucius, Mencius and Laozi?

(2) Do you think that people are still influenced by Confucianism and Taoism today? Give examples to illustrate your points.

Text C

The *Classic of Changes* (*Yijing*) and Its Place in Chinese Philosophy

The *Classic of Changes* (*Yijing*) is a complete edited work in two parts. One part is a manual of divination known simply as the Changes (*Yi*), or more correctly, as the *Zhouyi*. It is a handbook traceable to the period and practices of the Western Zhou dynasty as indicated, among other features, by its use of language expressions found on the bronzes of that period (BC 1046–771 BC). The other part of the *Classic of Changes* is a set of seven commentaries. Three of the commentaries are composed of two sections each. Taken as a whole, the commentary of this second part is known as "The Ten Wings" (*Shiyi*).

One of the commentaries is known as the *Great Commentary* (*Dazhuan*). It is arguably the most important text to study for an understanding of early Chinese ontology. The *Classic of Changes* as a whole is much less valuable for this purpose. Regrettably, a determinable date for the composition of the *Great Commentary* cannot be fixed. However, a version of it was discovered as a silk manuscript among the archaeological finds at the Mawangdui tomb site in Changsha in 1973. Therefore, it must be older than 168 BC when the tomb was closed. The work makes use of the fundamental philosophical vocabulary of Chinese ontology that continues to be used by Chinese thinkers up to the early modern period. It speaks of Heaven (*Tian*) and earth (*Di*) collectively (*TianDi*) as a way of talking about "reality". As for the process of reality's change, it employs the term *dao* as a nominative and portrays it as operating according patterns (*Tian Wen*) or Principle (s) (*Li*). In this commentary, the substance of reality (*Qi*) is capable of transforming into a myriad of experienced objects, evidencing properties of what might be called in the West "matter" or in other forms "spirit." *Qi* is moved by pushes and pulls of its internal opposing forces, *Yin and Yang* (*Great Commentary* Part I, 1, 4). Although reality's changes are not arbitrary, neither are they guided by a mind or divine intellect. The *Great Commentary* associates the patterns (*Li*) that give order to reality with the hexagrams found in the divination manual (the *Zhouyi*). The general philosophical term for the process of reality is "correlative ontology". Various correlations are possible; for example, *Yin and Yang* may be mutually supportive, or one may be transforming the other, balancing it, compensating for it, enhancing it, or furthering something new in relation to the other.

In Western philosophy, the characteristic approach to ontology is to think of things that compose reality as "natural kinds", each of which has a different essence that makes it what it is; for example, the essence of a chair, a cat, a tree, and so forth. This defining essence is typically called "the nature" of the object. In early Chinese ontology, change and process are more fundamental than continuity and endurance, even if there is sufficient constancy to speak of objects through time. The characteristic configuration of *qi* that something is actualizing sets it apart from other things. This distinctive correlation of *Yin* and *Yang* does the philosophical work of the Western concept of essence. It enables identification of kinds and categories of things, without recourse to an ontology in which there is a pluralism of essentially different sorts of substances.

Chinese philosophers inheriting the ontology of the *Yijing* and *Great Commentary* still use the concept of the "nature" of something, but "nature" does not refer to some underlying essence or immaterial substance that makes something what it is in distinction from other things. "Nature" is a way of talking about the manner of *qi* correlation that actualizes a thing as it is and sets it apart from the correlations of other things.

Vocabulary

manual *n.* 使用手册
configuration *n.* 结构；布局；形态
myriad *n.* 无数，极大数量
hexagram *n.* 六角星形
correlative *adj.* 有相互关系的；相关的
archaeological *adj.* ［古］考古学的；［古］考古学上的
ontology *n.* 本体论［技术］
nominative *n.* 任命
arbitrary *adj.* 随意的
pluralism *n.* 多元论

Exercises

1. Global reading

Decide whether the following statements are true (T) or false (F).

(1) The "*Classic of Changes*" traces back to the Western Zhou Dynasty.

(2) The *Great Commentary* (*Dazhuan*) can be considered as the most important text to study the early Chinese ontology.

(3) When talking about "reality", it mainly refers to Heaven (*Tian*) and earth (*Di*).

(4) The substance of reality (*Qi*) can transform into countless experienced objects, which is the same with the western "matter".

(5) *Yin* and *Yang* are completely opposing forces.

2. Questions for discussion

(1) What's the relationship between the substance of reality (*Qi*) in the Great Commentary and "matter" in the west?

(2) Can you give a brief introduction to *Yin* and *Yang* in your own words?

(3) What are the different approaches to ontology in western philosophy and in early Chinese philosophy?

3. Classroom activities

(1) Work in pairs and talk about the important place of "*Yijing*" in Chinese philosophy.

(2) Work in pairs and discuss the great influence that the fundamental philosophical vocabulary of Chinese ontology from the Great Commentary has on the Chinese thinkers of early modern periods.

Text D
Confucius: The Exemplary Person Ideal

The first access that most people have into Chinese philosophy in general, and certainly into the thought of Confucius, is through the *Analects* (*Lunyu*). This work is an anthology of selected sayings in which Confucius is often the main teacher. When speaking of morality, the term Confucius uses that is perhaps the closest in meaning is *Li*, often translated as the rites that guide conduct. *Li* refers to the manner of comporting oneself that helps people transcend animality, develop humaneness (*Ren*), and even exceed present ways of being human by raising themselves to higher expression. This expression is captured by the concept of "exemplary person" (*Junzi*).

In the *Analects*, the humane (*Ren*) person is able to endure hardship and enjoy happy circumstances, identify good and evil, and be free from the desire to do wrong. Being *Ren* comes through self-cultivation and observing *Li*, and it cannot be reduced to the dichotomy often found in Western moral theory between action (doing) and character (being). Confucius recognizes the importance of both what persons do and the sort of person one is. A person of *humane* character will act in a certain way; the construction of this character cannot occur without doing the *Li* acts derived from and embodied in the lives of persons who have gone before as our exemplars (*Junzi*). Making oneself into such a person is the work of self-cultivation.

There is no single word in the *Analects* for self-cultivation; but as a concept Confucius teaches, its imprint is present in the earliest stratum of his teachings. In thinking of the dedication and commitment needed for cultivating oneself, Confucius calls on his disciples to give their utmost (*Zhong*). Self-cultivation is not simply learning from books; it includes character development, enhancing talents, and refining (*Wen*) one's humanity itself. Cultivating oneself into an exemplary person is never merely reduced to one's moral actions or values. Confucius recognized that in the activity of self-cultivation everyone makes mistakes, but he taught that it is tragic to repeat a mistake or fail to reform after making one. Confucius thinks of human being development as taking a raw piece of jade and carving and polishing it until it is fully refined.

An exemplary person always does what is appropriate (*Yi*), cherishes moral excellence (*De*), and is not driven by desires. Exemplary persons take the high road, not the low one, and they feel ashamed if their high-sounding words are not fully reflected in their deeds. Indeed, exemplary persons cherish their excellence of character over power, land, or thought of gain. Exemplary persons take as much trouble discovering what is right as lesser men take to learn what will pay.

Confucius's teachings on the exemplary person and self-cultivation are the touchstone for the moral and human ideals of Chinese culture down to the present day.

Vocabulary

exemplary [ɪgˈzempləri] *adj.* 典范的；惩戒性的；可仿效的
anthology [ænˈθɒlədʒi] *n.* （诗、文、曲、画等的）选集
animality [ænɪˈmælɪtɪ] *n.* 兽性；人的动物本能；动物界；动物的生活
dichotomy [daɪˈkɒtəmi] *n.* 二分法；两分；分裂；双歧分枝
stratum [ˈstrɑːtəm] *n.* （组织的）层；[地质] 地层；社会阶层

Exercises

1. Global reading

Decide whether the following statements are true (T) or false (F).

(1) The *Analects* is an anthology of selected sayings said by Confucius.

(2) When speaking of morality, the term Confucius uses that is perhaps the closest in meaning is *De*.

(3) Confucius recognizes the importance of both what persons do and the sort of person one is. While in Western moral theory action (doing) and character (being) are divided.

(4) Self-cultivation is to refine one's moral actions or values.

(5) Exemplary persons never cherish their excellence of character over power, land, or thought of gain.

2. Questions for discussion

(1) Can you explain the Confucian doctrines of *Ren* and *Li* in your own words to each other?

(2) How do you understand self-cultivation in the *Analects*?

(3) What is the exemplary person ideal according to the passage?

3. Classroom activities

(1) Confucius thinks of human being development as taking a raw piece of jade and carving and polishing it until it is fully refined. Do you think people are born good or evil? Divide into two groups and have a debate.

(2) Choose several sentences you like from the *Analects* and share your understandings with your classmates.

Suggestions for Further Reading

Kujie Zhou. *A basic Confucius*. Long River Press, 2005.

Kujie Zhou. *A basic Dao: An Introduction to the Way*. Long River Press, 2009.

Unit 2 Chinese Food

People take food as their heaven, and food takes taste as its first.

——Chinese Proverb

Unit Goals

- To get familiar with Chinese eight regional cuisines, Chinese medicine food, Hotpot and traditional Chinese New Year food.
- To understand Chinese food culture.
- To learn useful words and expressions that relate to Chinese food and improve English languages skills.

Before You Read

1. Give the names of the following dishes.

2. Look at the pictures above and then discuss the following questions with your partners.

(1) What regional cuisines do they belong to?

(2) What are Chinese eight regional cuisines?

Intensive reading

Text A
Eight Regional Cuisines

China is a vast country with diverse climates, customs, products, and habits. Favored dishes vary from region. People in coastal areas prefer seafood and aquatic products, whereas those in central and northwest China eat more domestic animals and poultry. Foods vary from north to south. Tastes also differ regionally because of the climate differences. One popular summary of Chinese food is "sweet in the south, salty in the north, sour in the west and spicy in the east."

Despite differences in choices of dishes, people throughout the country adopt the traditional cooking style prevalent in their respective regions. Altogether, there are eight schools of cuisines: Shandong, Guangdong, Sichuan, Jiangsu, Zhejiang, Hunan, Anhui and Fujian cuisines. These regional cuisines have evolved over centuries, so their designations have no specific geographical boundaries.

Shandong Cuisine

Shandong Cuisine, known as Lu Cai, is representative of northern China's cooking and its techniques are widely practiced in northeast China. Consisting of Jinan cuisine and Jiaodong cuisine, Shandong Cuisine, clear, pure and not greasy, is characterized by its emphasis on aroma, freshness, crispness and tenderness. Shallot and garlic are usually used as seasonings so Shandong dishes tastes pungent usually. Soups are given much emphasis in Shandong dishes. Thin soup features clear and fresh while creamy soup looks thick and tastes strong. Jinan cuisine is adept at deep-frying, grilling, frying and stir-frying while Jiaodong division is famous for cooking seafood with fresh and light taste.

Sichuan Cuisine

Sichuan Cuisine, also known as Chuan Cai, is one of the most famous Chinese cuisines in the world. Characterized by its spicy and pungent flavor, Sichuan Cuisine, prolific of tastes, emphasizes on the use of chili. Pepper and prickly ash also never fail to accompany, producing typical exciting tastes. Besides, garlic, ginger and fermented soybean are also used in the cooking process. Wild vegetables are usually chosen as ingredients, while frying, frying without oil, pickling and braising are applied as basic cooking techniques.

Jiangsu Cuisine

Jiangsu Cuisine, also called Huaiyang Cuisine, is popular in the lower reach of the Yangtze River. Aquatics as the main ingredients, it stresses the freshness of materials. Its carving techniques are delicate, of which the melon carving technique is especially well known. Cooking techniques consist of stewing, braising, roasting, simmering, etc. The flavor of Huaiyang Cuisine is light, fresh and sweet and with delicate elegance. Jiangsu cuisine is well known for its careful selection of ingredients, its meticulous preparation methodology, and its not-too-spicy, not-too-bland taste. Since the seasons vary in climate considerably in Jiangsu, the cuisine also varies throughout the year. If the flavor is strong, it isn't too heavy; if light, not too bland.

Zhejiang Cuisines

Comprising local cuisines of Hangzhou, Ningbo and Shaoxing, Zhejiang Cuisine, not greasy, wins its reputation for freshness, tenderness, softness, smoothness of its dishes with mellow fragrance. Hangzhou Cuisine is the most famous one among the three. Precisely made, Hangzhou Cuisine boasts great variety, and favors quick-frying, frying, braising, and deep-frying; Ningbo Cuisine is salty and tasty, mainly cooked through steaming, roasting, and braising. The dishes are delicious, tender, soft and smooth. Shaoxing Cuisine is famous for river food. The dishes are tasty, crispy and soft and the soups are delicious and thick with rural flavors.

Guangdong Cuisine

Guangdong Cuisine is known as Yue Cai. Tasting clean, light, crisp and fresh, Guangdong Cuisine usually has fowl and other meats to produce its unique dishes. It has a wide and strict selection of ingredients and the cooking methods are mostly steaming, sautéing and stir-frying with thick gravy. Many kinds of porridges and refreshments provide enough nutrients to make up for the water lost through perspiration during the long, hot summer.

Hunan Cuisine

Hunan Cuisine or Xiang Cai is akin to that of the chili-rich Sichuan dishes. It is also characterized by a dense pungent flavor. Chili, pepper and shallot are necessities in this cuisine. Hunan Cuisine has hot and sour flavors, fresh aromas and deep colour. The local people eat hot peppers to help fight dampness and cold. The main cooking methods for Hunan dishes are braising, double-boiling, steaming and stewing. It is also renowned for its frequent use of preserved meat in cooking.

Fujian Cuisine

Fujian Cuisine is known as Min Cai. Fujian Cuisine was formed gradually through integration and exchanges between the Han culture of the central plains and ancient local Yue culture. Consisting of three distinct flavors of Fuzhou, Minnan and Minxi local dishes, Fujian Cuisine features light taste and tenderness, with sour and sweet tastes. The cooking puts great emphasis on choosing the choicest ingredients, and is thus particularly apt in preparing seafood dishes.

Anhui Cuisine

Anhui Cuisine, known as Hui Cai, is highly distinctive not only for its elaborate choices of cooking ingredients but also for its strict control of the cooking process. Anhui chefs pay great attention to the taste, color and cooking temperature of their dishes. They are particularly skilled at braising and stewing and are experts in cooking delicacies from the mountains and the sea. Anhui dishes preserve most of the original taste and nutrition of the ingredients. The food is slightly spicy and salty. Some master dishes are stewed in a heavy brown oily sauce. Ham and sugar are often added to improve the taste and enhance freshness.

The eight cuisines are not enough to cover all the different types of Chinese food. China is full of varieties of local food; even a small village or a country can have its own distinctive local dishes.

Vocabulary

aquatic *adj.* 水栖的；水生的

designation *n.* 名称；称号；称呼

aroma *n.* 芳香；香味

adept *adj.* 内行的；熟练的；擅长的

refreshment *n.* 食物和饮料

apt *adj.* 恰当的；适当的

meticulous *adj.* 细心的；小心翼翼地

domestic *adj.* 驯养的；作宠物饲养的；非野生的

prevalent *adj.* 流行的；普遍存在的；盛行的

cuisine *n.* 烹饪；风味；（通常指昂贵的饭店中的）饭菜，菜肴

poultry *n.* 家禽；禽的肉

greasy *adj.* （食物）油腻的

seasoning *n.* 调味品；作料

respective *adj.* 分别的；各自的

akin *adj.* 相似的；类似的

enhance *v.* 提高；增强；增进

After You Read

Exercises

1. Answer the following questions.

(1) What is one popular summary of Chinese food?
(2) What is the characteristic of Shandong Cuisine?
(3) What are the common seasonings in Sichuan Cuisine?
(4) What is Jiangsu Cuisine well known for?
(5) Why are there many kinds of porridge and refreshments in Guangdong Cuisine?

2. Fill in the blanks with the words given below. Change the form where necessary. Each word can be used only once.

cuisine	domestic	prevalent	respective	designation
aroma	adept	akin	apt	enhance

(1) The district is under consideration for ____________ as a conservation area.
(2) Kitzi was a (an) ____________ at getting people to talk confidentially to him.
(3) This is an opportunity to ____________ the reputation of the company.
(4) A ____________ animal is one that is not wild and is kept either on a farm to produce food or in someone's home as a pet.
(5) Listening to his life story is ____________ to reading a good adventure novel.
(6) The ____________ of a country or district is the style of cooking that is characteristic of that place.
(7) People are ____________ to confuse the two issues.
(8) They are each recognized specialists in their ____________ fields.
(9) The fruit owes its extraordinary ____________ to a mixture of three main chemicals.
(10) Despite the fact that the disease is so ____________, treatment is still far from satisfactory.

3. Decide whether the statements are true (T) or (F) according to the passage.

(1) The designations of eight regional cuisines have no specific geographical boundaries.

(2) Hangzhou Cuisine favors steaming, roasting, and braising.
(3) Hunan Cuisine has hot and sweet flavors, fresh aromas and light color.
(4) Fujian Cuisine features sour and sweet tastes.
(5) Anhui chefs are particularly skilled at deep-frying, grilling, frying and stir-frying.

4. Translation

(1) Jinan cuisine is adept at deep-frying, grilling, frying and stir-frying while Jiaodong division is famous for cooking seafood with fresh and light taste.
(2) Wild vegetables and animals are usually chosen as ingredients, while frying, frying without oil, pickling and braising are applied as basic cooking techniques.
(3) Comprising local cuisines of Hangzhou, Ningbo and Shaoxing, Zhejiang Cuisine, not greasy, wins its reputation for freshness, tenderness, softness, smoothness of its dishes with mellow fragrance.
(4) Fujian Cuisine was formed gradually through integration and exchanges between the Han culture of the central plains and ancient local Yue culture.
(5) Anhui Cuisine, known as Hui Cai, is highly distinctive not only for its elaborate choices of cooking ingredients but also for its strict control of the cooking process.

5. Pair work

Choose one cuisine form eight regional cuisines and describe its typical characteristics to your partner so that it can be guessed out. Then list at least two special dishes of this cuisine.

Read More
Extensive Reading

Text B
Chinese Medicine Food

The theory of *Yin* and *Yang* is applied to all Chinese things including the classification of food and herbs. For over three thousand years the Chinese have combined the various ingredients for cooking food and the various types of food in harmonious balance for sustenance and the improvement of health. Since the 5th century BC, they have discovered the secrets of using herbs and other natural ingredients for healing. The ancient records named *Huangdi Neijing* contain information on the anatomy of man, the causes of illnesses and the method of healing.

During the Three Kingdoms period the well-known physician, Hua Tuo, was skilled in applying a form of anesthesia for surgery. By the first century AD three thousand types of herbs were recorded in the *Shennong Bencaojing* for curing ailments. Ming dynasty physician Li Shizhen contributed much to the development of Chinese herbal medicine by compiling his voluminous *Bencao Gangmu* on 1892 types of Chinese herbs. His writings were translated into many foreign languages after publication.

To remain healthy a person needs fresh air, exercise, nourishing food and a healthy mental condition. Thus, the Chinese pay a great deal of attention to the way food is cooked and a balanced diet is maintained to sustain and prolong life. Chinese cuisine is a 3,000-year-old art based not only on skill and using the best quality ingredients but also on applying the ancient art of balancing the *Yin* and *Yang* qualities in the food. The Chinese classify each type of vegetable and meat in terms of *Yin* and *Yang*, and combine vegetables with meat in such a way that each cooked dish will be balanced. They know that food may be changed from one to the other depending on the way it is cooked.

For example, a steamed fish is *Yin* (cooling) but a deep fried fish is *Yang* (heating). The skill of balancing food was developed as early as the 16th century BC. A minister of the ruler of the Shang Kingdom named Yi created Chinese cooking utensils and the art of cooking using the nature of the food to balance the diet.

During the 5th century BC cooks began to create cuisines with medical values. In the publication called *Huangdi Neijing*, a Warring States record, there are rules on how to regulate diet and improve the taste of food. The *Han* publication, *Shennong Bencaojing*, listed certain herbs and vegetables as being beneficial to the body.

By the Song Dynasty it was recorded that many diseases could be cured through proper diet and eating the right food. The development of cooking skills and lists of food for curing ailments intensified during the *Jin*, *Yuan* and *Qing* Dynasties. Different foods were classified according to their perceived nature. They might be *han* (cold/*Yin*), *liang* (cool/*Yin*), *ping* (neutral), *wen* (slightly warm/*Yang*) and *re* (hot/*Yang*). *Han* and *liang* foods were believed to reduce fever, relieve thirstiness and coughs while *wen*, warm foods reduce running noses, headache, etc.

The five tastes of food are sour, sweet, bitter, hot and salty. Sour food relieves diarrhoea, asthma and other disorders. Slightly sweet food relieves ailments connected with the veins. Bitter food helps to cure an overheated body system. Hot food helps blood circulation and salty food helps to stop diarrhoea.

Han food (cold food) includes bitter gourd, lotus, water melon, sugar cane, tomato, banana, dong gourd, yellow gourd, snail, crab, etc. *Liang* food (cold food) includes radish, towel gourd, maize, green bean, bean curd, orange, apple, pear, duck egg, abalone, frog's leg, mushroom, etc. *Han* and *Liang* food such as abalone regulates the liver function because it cools the "*yangness*" in the system. Hot food is chilli, pepper and other foods with a hot taste.

Wen food (mild food) includes apricot, ginger, spring onion, onion, papaya, glutinous rice, wine, vinegar, almond, dates, venison, prawn, fish, chicken meat, beef, goat meat, liver, ham, etc. *Wen* and hot food such as apricot stimulates blood circulation and nurtures the heart and lungs.

The neutral or *ping* food includes rice, sweet potato, flat bean, yellow bean, black bean, red bean, red carrot, ground nut, lotus seed, corn, pomfret, fruit, pork, goose meat, frog meat, butter and milk and these foods nourish the spleen and balance the digestive system.

Knowing the nature of individual foods enables the Chinese to eat the proper food to nurture the various internal organs, balance the *Yin* and *Yang*, and enhance the *Qi* of the body.

For example, to nurture the stomach they believe one should eat carrots, melons, apples and vegetables. To nourish the spleen one can drink honey and drinks made from herbs prescribed by a Chinese medicine shop.

Vocabulary

classification *n.* 分类；归类；分级

sustenance *n.* 食物；营养；养料

anesthesia *n.* 麻醉

prolong *v.* 延长

diarrhea *n.* 腹泻

ingredient *n.* 成分；（尤指烹饪）原料

anatomy *n.* 人体

ailment *n.* 轻病；小恙

utensil *n.* （家庭）用具，器皿；家什

asthma *n.* 气喘；哮喘

beneficial *adj.* 有利的；有裨益的；有用的

intensify *v.* 加强，增强，加剧

Exercises

1. Global Reading

Decide whether the following statements are true (T) or false (F).

(1) The Chinese already found out the secrets of using herbs and other natural ingredients for healing more than 2500 years ago.

(2) To live longer, the Chinese pay more attention to the balanced diet than the cooking ways of the food.

(3) The *Yin and Yang* qualities in the food can't be changed from one to the other by the cooking ways.

(4) The Chinese have developed the skill of balancing food for no more than 3000 years.

(5) The Chinese eat food on the basis of the nature of individual foods so as to balance the *Yin and Yang* and enhance the *Qi* of the body.

2. Questions for discussion

(1) Review and discuss the development of Chinese medicine food in the history.

(2) How many ancient medical records are mentioned in the passage and what are their respective contributions?

(3) How many kinds can the food be divided into according to their perceived nature? What are their functions for healing?

3. Classroom activities

(1) Search for some legends about the Chinese medicine food and choose one to share it with the class.

(2) According to the *Yin and Yang* qualities of the food, which kinds of food should people eat in different seasons?

Text C
Hotpot Culture in China

"The nation is so crazy about hotpot that people are willing to line up for hours to get in their favorite hotpot restaurants!" Many foreigners find it rather interesting and many of them cannot understand such a craze about hotpot, which is not only a kind of food but also a lifestyle, even a culture in China.

Why Chinese like eating hotpot?

The hotpot has a long history of over 1,000 years in China. It used to be favored only in winter, but recently it appears on tables all year round. Besides its delicious flavor, there are two other important reasons for the deep affinity with hotpot of Chinese people.

The first one is that it is a great way for family gatherings. In Chinese culture, red stands for joyousness and round for family gathering. Therefore, culturally, red, round hotpot is a visual symbol of warm, enthusiasm and family gathering. Family gatherings are a crucial component of Chinese culture. Chinese people love to gather with their friends or family, especially in the winter, sitting around a big round dining table, eating and chatting over a steaming pot in the middle with their favorite dishes surrounding them.

The other is that hotpot is a kind of "healthy meal". Boiling is better than frying, and bone nutrients are released into the broth. Eating hotpot can warm the body and improve blood circulation in winter, and increase perspiration to help cool the body in summer. Some seasonings in hotpot can help alleviate minor illnesses like a cold, a stuffy nose or headaches.

What are different types of hotpot by region?

There are several varieties of hotpot in China with differently flavored broth. Two of the most popular hotpot are Sichuan hotpot and Beijing mutton hotpot (instant-boiled mutton). Some other popular ones include seafood hotpot in Guangdong, sauerkraut hotpot in northeast China, chrysanthemum hotpot in Suzhou and beef hotpot in Hong Kong. Besides, its name varies a lot by region—in Guangdong it is called "*Bian Lu*" (边炉), in Ningxia "*Guo Zi*" (锅子), in Jiangsu and Zhejiang "*Nuan Guo*" (暖锅), and in Sichuan "*Huo Guo*" (火锅).

Debates over Chengdu hotpot and Chongqing hotpot.

Chengdu and Chongqing are two of the most famous hotpot cities in China. For anyone going to Chengdu and Chongqing, eating a delicious hotpot should be on their to-do-list. However, there have always been debates over which is authentic or not.

Chengdu hotpot is famous for its numbing and spicy flavor, resulting from a special seasoning—Sichuan pepper (花椒), and other spicy ingredients like chili, which makes the hotpot distinct from others. While Chongqing hotpot is characterized by hotness, heavy flavors and dense soup, its traditional materials include cattle guts, cattle waists, beef and other vegetables and is, a real self-help course. As a matter of fact, both Chengdu hotpot and Chongqing hotpot come from the same origin. It is hard to say which is authentic, it's simply up to you.

Nowadays, along with the development of cooking techniques, hotpot has gained more varieties and characteristics. It will not only reflect China's profound history, but also represent modern Chinese culture. Whenever you come to China, especially to Chongqing or Chengdu, you should try this popular Chinese dish.

Vocabulary

affinity *n.* 喜好；喜爱
broth *n.*（加入蔬菜的）肉汤，鱼汤
perspiration *n.* 汗；汗珠
sauerkraut *n.*（酸）泡菜
authentic *adj.* 真正的；真品的；真迹的
numbing *adj.* 令人麻木的；使人失去知觉的
visual *adj.* 视力的；视觉的
alleviate *v.* 减轻；缓和；缓解
stuffy *adj.*（鼻子）不通的，堵塞的
chrysanthemum *n.* 菊花

Exercises

1. Global reading

Decide whether the following statements are true（T）or false（F）.

(1) The craze of Chinese people about hotpot makes many foreigners feel confused.
(2) Now hotpot is a favorite food all year round.
(3) It isn't very healthy to eat hotpot in summer because it lets people sweat more.
(4) Hotpot in China is classified into different kinds according to the regions.
(5) Chengdu hotpot, different from Chongqing hotpot, is characterized by its spicy and heavy flavors with dense soup.

2. Questions for discussion

(1) Why is hotpot so popular in China?
(2) How is hotpot classified in China? And what are the popular hotpot?
(3) What are the main distinctions between Chengdu hotpot and Chongqing hotpot?

3. Classroom activities

(1) Search for more information about the history of hotpot and share your findings with your partner.

(2) Choose your favorite kind of hotpot and make a presentation about its history, characteristics, traditional materials, etc. ?

Text D

Traditional Chinese New Year Food

What do you eat for your Christmas dinner? Do you eat Stuffing turkey, ham, apple pies or fruitcakes? Correspondingly, what do Chinese people eat for celebrating their Chinese New Year?

Just like Christmas dinner in Western countries, the family reunion dinner on Chinese New Year's Eve matters a lot for Chinese people. It is a grand occasion for the family to come together and share the happy time.

The dishes served for dinner, however, vary in different areas of China. Generally, we say the Northerners love pasta while the Southerners prefer rice. But when it comes to the family banquet for Chinese New Year, things seem to get more complicated.

1. Steamed Fish: Always Have More Than You Wish For

Fish is one of the main dishes commonly eaten for the New Year dinner throughout the whole country; fish is "余 (*yú*) " in Chinese, a word symbolizing surplus. So eating fish stands for: "always have more than you wish for".

It is important that the fish is served with the head and tail intact to ensure a good start and finish, and to avoid bad luck throughout the year. The general way to cook fish is to either steam or braise it.

2. Chicken: Good Luck!

Chicken "*jī*" (鸡) is a homophone for "吉 (*jí*) ", which means good luck and auspice in Chinese culture.

Some places where there are well-preserved traditional customs will serve a whole chicken on the dinner table to show happiness and reunion.

Chicken dishes for family reunion dinner including:

In northeast of China: stewed chicken with mushrooms

Shanghai: drunk chicken.

Chengdu: braised rooster.

In south of China (Guilin, Guangzhou, Hong Kong): cantonese poached chicken, chicken soup.

3. Pork: Prosperous Life

In rural areas of China, it is a tradition to kill a domestic pig for the Spring Festival, to comfort a year's hard work. People who don't raise pigs regard eating pork at family reunion dinner as a symbol of rich life.

In northeast of China: double cooked pork slices.

Beijing: braised pork balls in gravy.

Shanghai: Shanghai-style braised pork belly, sweet and sour spare ribs.

In south of China (Guilin, Guangzhou, Hong Kong): *mei cai kou rou* (Steamed Pork with Preserved Mustard), *char siu* (Chinese BBQ pork).

4. Shrimp: Laugh Out Loud Every Day

Your mouth will look like you are saying "*hahaha*" when saying shrimp, "*xiā* 虾" in Chinese. People eat shrimp at this most important dinner to wish a happy life for the coming New Year.

In northeast of China: braised prawns.

Shanghai: sautéed shelled shrimps.

In south of China (Guilin, Guangzhou, Hong Kong): scalded (boiled) prawns.

5. Dumplings: Changes from the Old and to the New

Dumplings, "*jiǎo zi* (饺子)" in Chinese, sound like "*jiāo zǐ*" (交子), a must-eat side dish in northern China, which means changes from the old and to the new. Because it is shaped similar to a gold ingot, eating dumplings on New Year's Eve also has the meaning of "ushering in wealth and prosperity".

What's interesting is that people who eat the dumplings occasionally stuffed with special materials like a coin, a candy, a peanut or a red date, will have the best luck in the New Year.

6. *Tang Yuan*: Family Reunion

Tang Yuan-sweet soup with balls-is a symbol of family reunion in Chinese culture. Corresponding to the Northerners eating dumplings, the Southerners are used to eating *Tang Yuan* on New Year's Eve, which shows the wishes of happiness and reunion.

7. Spring Rolls: Ten Thousand Taels of Gold

Spring rolls—*Chun Juan* or *Chun Bing* in Chinese—are golden fried pastries from the south of China, with those from Shanghai and Guangdong being the best known.

The name is intrinsically linked to the Spring Festival. The Chinese have had the custom of having spring rolls since ancient times, to mark the end of winter and to welcome a lively spring.

8. Vegetables: Hardworking and Make Fortune

The Chinese New Year dinner is mostly meat-based. Of course it needs some embellishments. Every dish served for the dinner has a special purpose, and vegetables have no exception.

(1) Celery, "*qín cài* (芹菜)", "*qín* (芹)" pronounced the same as "*qín* (勤)", which means hardworking in Chinese. It represents that parents hope their kids to work hard in the New Year.

(2) Lettuce, "*xiāng cài*" is similar to "make fortune" in Cantonese. Lettuce is cooked with oyster sauce and sprinkled with some fried mashed garlic, a dish meaning "gold bars make fortune".

(3) Garlic chives, "*jiǔ cài* 韭菜", "*jiǔ* (韭)" sounds the same with "*jiǔ* (久)", which means long and everlasting in Chinese. So eating garlic chives at Chinese New Year means: "good days will be long-lasting".

9. Desserts: Nian Gao

Nian Gao, New Year's cake or rice cake, sounds like "getting higher year by year" in Chinese. The higher you are, the more prosperous your business is. Hence the Year Cake symbolizes achieving new heights in the coming year.

Vocabulary

reunion *n.* 重聚,(亲友等的)聚会
complicated *adj.* 结构复杂的
intact *adj.* 原封不动的;完好无缺
auspice *n.* 预兆;前兆;吉兆
usher *v.* 引领,招待
intrinsically *adv.* 从本质上(讲)
pasta *n.* 面团
surplus *adj.* 过剩的;多余的
homophone *n.* 同音异义词
burgeon *v.* 发芽,抽枝;迅速发展
tael *n.* 两,银两
embellishment *n.* 装饰,修饰

Exercises

1. Global reading

Decide whether the following statements are true (T) or false (F).

(1) The dishes served for dinner on Chinese New Year's Eve are similar in different areas of China.

(2) Fish is one of common food eaten for the New Year dinner all over China.

(3) A whole chicken is served on the dinner table to ensure a good start and finish in some places.

(4) Dumplings have the meaning of changing from the old and to the new.

(5) Having spring rolls on Spring Festive is a new custom for Chinese people.

2. Questions for discussion

(1) Why does the dinner on Chinese New Year's Eve matter a lot for Chinese people?

(2) What good wishes do people make by eating these food?

(3) Which food in the passage is popular in the north of China? And which is popular in the South? What are the differences between them?

3. Classroom activities

(1) What food do you eat in your home on the Spring Festival? What meaning does the food have?

(2) What food do you know Chinese people eat on other traditional festivals? Choose one traditional festival and introduce the food eaten on this festival.

Suggestion for Further Reading

Liu Junru. Chinese Food. China: *Intercontinental communication center*, 2017.

Unit 3 Chinese Tea

It's always said that a good cup of tea is somewhat like a beauty.

——Chinese Poem

Unit Goals

- To introduce Chinese tea briefly.
- To get familiar with the customs of drinking tea.
- To learn the teahouse culture in China.
- To learn useful words and expressions that relate to Chinese tea and improve English languages skills.

Before You Read

1. Describe what you have known from the following pictures.

2. Look at the pictures above and then discuss the following questions with your partners.

(1) Briefly tell the origin of traditional Chinese Tea.

(2) Name some well-known tea and share one kind with your partner.

Intensive Reading

Text A
A Brief Introduction to Chinese Tea

Being a vivid Chinese cultural specialty as well as *Kungfu* and traditional Chinese medicine, Chinese tea has been being developed in China for a long time accompanied with which a series of tea culture took shape. Widely known in Chinese history as a fortuitous discovery of *Shennong* (神农), a renowned Chinese legendary chieftain and respected physician in the far ancient times, tea had been mentioned in the old Chinese medical work "Herbal Classic (本草经) ", which was written in the 1st century.

"Tea Classic", the first work about tea in the world written by Lu Yu (733-804, the "Chinese Tea Saint" living in Tang Dynasty), represents that not only did Chinese tea play an essential part in diet but also tea culture seeped into all aspects of people's daily life, e. g. poetry, painting, calligraphy, religion, medicine. Nowadays in China a great deal of knowledge about tea is still treated as invaluable patrimony, tea is still a common drink on the table and it has even become an ideal present when people host or visit others.

Used as medicine at the very beginning and then cooked with other food as diet, tea was not made by soaking tea-leaves with hot water until Ming Dynasty (1368-1644), which is the most common way of making tea in China today. However, there are still some differences in making teas due to the varieties of the tea-leaves. It is a common sense to make a cup of tea by filling hot water into the cup with instant or small-bag tea-leaves, but it is widely considered to be a better way to make mellow tea by soaking tea-leaves with hot water in a teapot for some time (5-10 minutes or longer, depending on personal preference). Tea-leaves are usually discarded after being soaked once or twice.

In China nowadays, tea still plays an important role in people's daily life especially at home, restaurants and teahouses. Generally, elders are fond of the traditional tea-making for leisure and the original taste, while the youth prefer bottled tea drinks because of its convenience and various flavors.

Vocabulary

seep *v.* 渗透
renowned *adj.* 著名的；有声望的
accompany *v.* 陪伴；伴随
chieftain *n.* 首领
instant *adj/n.* 立即的；瞬间
essential *adj/n.* 必不可少的；本质
host *n/v.* 主人；主办
mellow *adj.* 芳醇的
specialty *n.* 专业
fortuitous *adj.* 偶然的
physician *n.* 医师，内科医生
patrimony *n.* 遗产
flavor *n/v.* 滋味；给……调味

After You Read

Exercises

1. Answer the following questions.

(1) What are the three Chinese cultural specialties?
(2) When did the old Chinese medical work "Herbal Classic（本草经）" come into being?
(3) Who wrote the "Tea Classic"?
(4) Which dynasty was tea made by soaking tea-leaves with hot water?
(5) Why does the youth prefer bottled tea drinks?

2. Fill in the blanks with the words given below. Change the form where necessary. Each word can be used only once.

specialty	accompany	essential	host	seep
herbal	mellow	due to	original	calligraphy

(1) His ____________ is vigorous and forceful.
(2) Try to catch the elusive charm of the____________ in translation.
(3) The car collision succeeded on the expressway____________ a dense fog.
(4) The wine tastes ____________.
(5) On the other hand they can try____________ teas to relax.
(6) If Mr Saleh cannot soon bring a modicum of prosperity to his people, the spirit of revolt may ____________ into his own back yard.

(7) Mr. Marce will ____________ a reception tonight.

(8) They believe it is ____________ to defy convention.

(9) If she sang, he would ____________ her on the piano.

(10) Wood carving are a ____________ of this village.

3. Decide whether the statements are true (T) or (F) according to the passage.

(1) The old Chinese medical work "Herbal Classic (本草经)" was written in the 1st century.

(2) "Tea Classic" is not the first work about tea in the world written by *Lu Yu*.

(3) Chinese tea is a vivid Chinese cultural specialty as well as *Kungfu* and traditional Chinese medicine.

(4) Tea was made by soaking tea-leaves with hot water at the very beginning.

(5) Generally, elders are fond of the traditional tea-making for leisure and the original taste.

4. Translation

(1) Being a vivid Chinese cultural specialty as well as *Kungfu* and traditional Chinese medicine, Chinese tea has been being developed in China for a long time accompanied with which a series of tea culture took shape.

(2) "Tea Classic" represents that not only did Chinese tea play an essential part in diet but also tea culture seeped into all aspects of people's daily life, e. g. poetry, painting, calligraphy, religion, medicine.

(3) Tea-leaves are usually discarded after being soaked once or twice.

(4) In China nowadays, tea still plays an important role in people's daily life especially at home, restaurants and teahouses.

(5) Nowadays in China a great deal of knowledge about tea is still treated as invaluable patrimony, tea is still a common drink on the table and it has even become an ideal present when people host or visit others.

5. Pair work

Read a well-known book about Chinese tea and tell your partner about the book in English. And then Share the book and comments with the class.

Read More
Extensive Reading

Text B
Customs of Drinking Tea

China has the earliest history of drinking tea. Therefore, Chinese people know best the true interest in drinking tea. When guests call in they are entertained with tea. Substituting tea for wine and gifts has been the doctrine of drinking tea for all nationalities in our country through the ages.

Han nationality: The Han nationality has a long history of drinking tea in varied ways. They generally prefer green tea, scented tea, black tea or Wulong tea. Most of them have a liking for unadulterated drinks. They believe that only through unadulterated drinks can they best appreciate and taste the serenity, elegance and verve of tea. Drinking medicinal tea is not aimed at "tasting", but rather at experiencing its effects on medical and health care.

Zang nationality: The Zang people are very proficient in the nutrition deployment of tea drinking. They like butter tea the best. This tea has a rich taste with sweetness and saltiness amid acerbity, as well as a permeating fragrance. It has the effects of warming up the body and resisting the cold. Butter tea is regarded as a special product. When a couple holds a wedding ceremony, tea is used as a symbol of a happy and contented marriage.

Uygur nationality: The Uygur people revel in drinking tea and regard it as important as rice. There is a popular saying in Xinjiang: "I would rather take no rice than no tea in a day." They like milk tea and fragrant tea the best.

Mongolian nationality: The Mongolian people like salty milk tea, which is made by mixing tea, milk and salt. The boiling of the tea seems simple, but in fact it involves certain techniques. Generally, when a girl is old enough, she learns them from her mother. During the wedding ceremony she performs the art of boiling tea in public and presents it to the guests to show that she has unusual skills and has been well educated at home.

China is a nation with numerous nationalities. The history, culture and geographical environment of all nationalities vary and their customs of drinking tea are also very colorful and have their own strong points. There is the Bamboo Tube Fragrant Tea of the Dai nationality, the Yanba tea and Dragon and Tiger tea of the Naxi nationality, the

Thunder Tea of the Lisu nationality, the Lei Tea of the Tujia nationality, the Sour Tea of the Bulang nationality, the Three-course Tea of the Bai nationality, the Oil Tea of the Miao nationality and the Jar Tea of the Hui nationality in Yunnan, etc. They are too numerous to mention one by one and all have their own characteristics.

Vocabulary

doctrine *n.* 主义；学说；教义；信条
nationality *n.* 国籍；民族
serenity *n.* 平静，宁静；晴朗，风和日丽
proficient *adj.* 熟练的，精通的
fragrant *adj.* 芳香的；愉快的
scented *adj.* 有香味的；有气味的；洒了香水的
entertain *v.* 娱乐；招待；怀抱；容纳
substitute *v.* 替代
verve *n.* 热情；神韵；活力；气魄
acerbity *n.* 酸，涩；刻薄
contented *adj.* 满足的

Exercises

1. Global reading

Decide whether the following statements are true（T）or false（F）.

（1）Substituting tea for wine and gifts has been the doctrine of drinking tea for all nationalities in our country through the ages.

（2）For the Han nationality, drinking medicinal tea is not only aimed at "tasting", but also at experiencing its effects on medical and health care.

（3）The Zang people are very proficient in the nutrition deployment of tea drinking.

（4）There is a popular saying in the Mongolian people: "I would rather take no rice than no tea in a day."

（5）The Mongolian people like salty milk tea, which is made by mixing tea, milk and salt.

2. Questions for discussion

（1）When guests call in, what has been the doctrine for all nationalities in our country through the ages?

（2）What kind of tea does the Han nationality generally prefer?

（3）China is a nation with numerous nationalities. How can their customs of drinking tea vary?

3. Classroom activities

(1) Can you name the different customs of numerous nationalities in China?

(2) What are characteristics for the Mongolian nationality in making tea?

Text C
Teahouse Culture in China

Teahouse has been ranked as the public place for drinking tea, relaxation and entertainment since ancient times, acting as a vivid epitome of Chinese tea culture and Chinese people's leisure lives. Besides providing a place for drinking tea, Chinese teahouses constantly launch new varieties in order to meet different needs of various people. In winter, tonics with the effectiveness of keeping bodies warm are added into the tea. In summer, something with the effectiveness of driving away summer heat is added in the tea. Besides, in summer, some cold drinks are also sold in teahouses, such as sweet bean paste, cocoribe, stewed plum water and papaya juice. As for tea sets, there are custom-made tea sets varying from different kinds of tea, revealing the rich and long-standing culture of teahouses in China.

Chinese teahouse culture prospered in the Song Dynasty, with teahouses all over cities and villages, when teahouses were as many as restaurants. In the Ming and Qing Dynasties, the number of the teahouses exceeded that of restaurants, becoming more popular and famous. The owners of teahouses in the Song Dynasty preferred to decorate their teahouses with calligraphy and painting of celebrities and various rare and precious plants, in order to attracting customers. In the Qing Dynasty, with the acculturation of western culture, teahouses of China took on new look. Teahouses could be found in the beautiful suburb, by the pool and in the vineyard, providing a peace and quiet place for drinking tea as well as enjoying the natural scenery in every season. Besides, some magnificent western-style teahouses occurred during that period.

Chinese teahouses enjoy a long-standing history, dating back to the Tang and Song Dynasties. Chinese teahouses originated in the Western Jin Dynasty, took shape in the Tang Dynasty and developed and completed in the Song, Yuan, Ming and Qing Dynasties. It became prosperous in the modern times and early years after liberation. In the contemporary era, it becomes glorious. The developing courses of teahouse reveal the developing condition of economy, society and culture in certain period.

After reform and opening-up, with the rapid development of economy and improvement of people's living standards, teahouses flourished in China. According to the statistics, there have been more than 25,000 teahouses in China, with the employees of over 2,500,000.

Teahouses of Beijing boasts high grade, among which, there are teahouses with the minimum charge of 1,000 Yuan per person; while Shanghai teahouses feature large quantity.

Vocabulary

epitome *n.* 缩影；象征
tonics *n.* 奎宁水
plum *n.* 梅子
reveal *v.* 透露；暴露；揭露
exceed *v.* 超过；胜过；优于
acculturation *n.* 文化适应
prosperous *adj.* 兴旺的
magnificent *adj.* 壮丽的；华丽的；极好的
launch *n.* 发射；发起
stewed *v.* 炖的；煮酥的；汁浓味苦的
papaya *n.* 番木瓜
prosper *v.* 富足；兴旺
celebrities *n.* 名誉；名人
vineyard *n.* 葡萄园
charge *n.* 要价；费用

Exercises

1. Global reading

Decide whether the following statements are true（T）or false（F）.

(1) In summer, some cold drinks are not sold in teahouses.

(2) There are custom-made tea sets varying from different kinds of tea, revealing the rich and long-standing culture of teahouses in China.

(3) In the Ming and Qing Dynasties, the number of the teahouses did not exceeded that of restaurants.

(4) Some magnificent western-style teahouses occurred during the Qing Dynasty.

(5) Besides providing a place for drinking tea, Chinese teahouses constantly launch new varieties in order to meet different needs of various people.

2. Questions for discussion

(1) In the Qing Dynasty, with the acculturation of western culture, how did the teahouses of China take on new look?

(2) When did Chinese teahouse culture prosper?

(3) Why did teahouses flourish in China after reform and opening-up?

3. Classroom activities

(1) Work in pairs and discuss: How do you understand Teahouse Culture in China.

(2) Can you give an example o illustrate the developing process of Teahouse Culture in China.

Text D

Across China: Tea Art Brightens Life of Left-behind Children

Changsha, July 14 (Xinhua) ——Jiang Birou, 19, still remembers the excitement she had experienced when attending her first tea ceremony class as a sixth-grade student. "That was my first extra-curricular class," Jiang said, adding that tea ceremony had brightened her childhood.

Located in the midst of mountains at a high altitude, Jiang's hometown in Weishan Township, central China's Hunan province, has favorable conditions for tea plantation but is marred with less arable land and inconvenient transportation. As a result, a large number of youths migrate to cities for better job opportunities, leaving behind their children and parents.

Jiang was once such a left-behind child. "When I was a little girl, I used to help my grandparents pick tea leaves, and I didn't have much communication with my parents." The change came in 2012 when Jiang's school organized a slew of extra-curricular activities and Jiang was the first to sign up for the tea ceremony class.

"In Weishan, almost every household grows tea, but we know little about the traditional tea culture," Jiang said. "Through the tea class, however, I learned a lot."

"In retrospect, I feel the tea art classes helped me calm my mind, manage my emotions and I began to communicate more with my parents because of the interesting classes," she said. Jiang is now a freshman at Wuhan Conservatory of Music. Due to the COVID-19, the commencement of her new semester got delayed, and she stayed in Weishan for a protracted Spring Festival holiday. During this time, she often visited her alma mater. Jiang said the sight of primary school girls learning tea art in a clean and bright classroom, makes her proud. "I hope they can enjoy the tea ceremony, as it will bring more harvests than they could imagine."

Eleven-year-old Gao Yingxin has been attending tea art classes for a year. Once a shy and reserved girl, she can now open her heart and make many good friends. "The gestures and movements we learn in the class are very interesting, so is the costume we wear," Gao said. A blissful smile blooms over Gao's face at the mention of the tea ceremony. She said tea-related activities such as plucking leaves and discussing tea-making, enriched her extra-curricular life. When talking to her father who works in India by phone, she would share stories about her tea art classes. Gao is among the 27 students currently taking the tea art class in the school, and about 85 percent of her classmates are left-behind children.

According to Principal Yang Jinpeng, the school has offered tea art classes to students in grades three to six since 2012, with more than 30 students signing up each year.

"Many children become more optimistic and confident after joining the tea art classes," Yang said. "We hope that through tea art and other extra-curricular classes, children can forge companionship with their classmates and teachers and learn something meaningful."

Vocabulary

curricular *adj.* 课程的
brighten *v.* （使）更明亮，色彩鲜艳；（使）有希望
favorable *adj.* 赞同的，令人愉快的
arable *adj.* 耕作的
household *n/adj.* 家庭、一家人/家庭的
retrospect *n/vt.* &*vi.* 回想/回顾/追溯
calm *adj/v/n.* 镇静的/使平静/平静的时期
epidemic *n/adj.* 流行病/流行性的
protracted *adj.* 延长的
reserved *adj/v.* 内向的/保留、预订
blissful *adj.* 极乐的，幸福的
bloom *n/v.* 花、有精神的面貌/开花、变得健康
forge *v/n.* 伪造、制作/铁匠铺、锻造工厂
companionship *n.* 友情，友谊
mar *n/v.* 瑕疵/破坏

Exercises

1. Global reading
Decide whether the following statements are true（T）or false（F）.

（1）Jiang Birou, once as a sixth-grade student, said that the tea ceremony class was her first extra-curricular class.

(2) Jiang's hometown in Weishan Township, central China's Hunan Province, isn't favorable for tea plantation.

(3) In Weishan, almost every household grows tea, and they know much about the traditional tea culture.

(4) Gao Yingxin thinks that the gestures and movements they learn in the class are very interesting, so is the costume they wear.

(5) Principal Yang hope that through tea art and other extra-curricular classes, children can forge companionship with their classmates and teachers.

2. Questions for discussion

(1) In Jiang's hometown, Weishan Township, why do a large number of youths migrate to cities for better job opportunities, leaving behind their children and parents?

(2) What did she usually do, when Jiang was a little girl, as once such a left-behind child?

(3) How has the tea art classes changed the eleven-year-old Gao Yingxin ?

3. Classroom activities

Work in pairs and discuss:

(1) What can you learn from attending the tea ceremony class.

(2) According to Principal Yang Jinpeng, summarize the benefits tea art classes offered to students in grades three to six since 2012.

Suggestion for Further Reading

Liutong. Chinese Tea. translated by Yue Liwen, Beijing: Foreign Languages Press, 2010.

Unit 4 Chinese Traditional Architecture

Beauty lies in the combination of natural landscape and artistic.

——Luis Barragan

Unit Goals

- To get familiar with the features of the Chinese traditional architecture.
- To get familiar with art of the Chinese traditional architecture.
- To understand the implication of totems of the Chinese traditional architecture.
- To learn useful words and expressions that relates to the Chinese traditional architecture and improve English languages skills.

Before You Read

1. Give the names of the following traditional architectures according to the pictures.

2. Look at the pictures above and then discuss the following questions with your partners.

(1) Briefly tell the features of the Chinese traditional architecture.

(2) Name a few well-known Chinese traditional architecture and share one story with your partner.

Intensive Reading

Text A
Art of the Chinese Traditional Architecture

If you have been to the Forbidden City, you will be attracted by the great city which has all of wonders and splendors of the ancient China. It is not only the biggest palace in the world, but also the greatest architectural art in the world. In China, building is not just a kind of technology, and it is also an art. How are the artistic expressions in the Chinese traditional construction? From an architectural perspective, ancient Chinese people show the construction's artistry from rich decorative roofs, the application of the background building and the use of colors.

Chinese architecture is a style of architecture, which has formed many centuries in Eastern Asia. Construction principles of Chinese architecture have remained largely unchanged; the only major change is the decorative architectural details. Chinese architecture is a particularly beautiful branch of the Chinese civilization; it creates a unique, outstanding traditional Chinese culture. The architecture of China is as old as Chinese civilization. From the literary, graphics, templates and a series of information sources that the Chinese people always use the indigenous system of construction, retained the main architectural features, from prehistoric times to the present. Through the Tang and Song Dynasties, Chinese architecture retained the basic characteristics that had already developed in the Han Dynasty, although there was a greater technical mastery and a tendency toward rich adornment and complexity of the system of bracketing.

The rich decorative roofs. In Chinese architecture, roof is a very important part. It not only has long history, beautiful looking, but also has a deep meaning. Long before, the Chinese architects found they could use the roofs to make an artistic effect. In "The Book of Songs", a very famous Chinese ancient poetries' anthology, there are some poetries coping with the people's life, and there are some poetries about roofs. That is to say, before 3,000 years, the Chinese poets had praised the beautiful roofs stretch as wing. So, the roofs' style have developed in China for a long time. The Chinese ancient people made full use of the characteristic of the roofs. They invented rising wall and turning up roof. It makes the eaves to form such as bird's wing and makes the soft beautiful curve to the every part of the roof. At that time, they made the comfortable incising on the ridge, and the tiles were made by the sculpture. Chinese people want the building into the nature, and hope the roof that can become a part of the environment. Sometimes, the curved roofs have another deep meaning. For example, temple roofs do not use straight line because the Buddhist believed that it could help them ward off evil spirits. Chinese people use those beautiful roofs to show the uniqueness about Chinese traditional construction.

The back ground building. Compared with western architecture, much of traditional Chinese architecture includes many adjunctive buildings. It seems to be a kind of building complex. In China, building complexes include main building, background building and environment. It becomes a building system, so it must have an optimum space. The relationship between main building and background building is like the relationship between flowers and green leaves. If there is not main building, the building complex does not have its function, and if there is not background building, it will be tedium and does not have a rich visual experience. So the background building can make the integral feeling become regular and full of changes, and show the building complex level of flu. In the ancient Chinese palaces or temples, using background building to show the art and beauty are very common. The background building must set off the main building. The earliest artistic background building is "Que". For instance, a watch tower on the either side of a palace gate or tomb passage. The form and the grave about this building are very beautiful and fine. After Ming Dynasty, it was developed to a great gate, such as the Meridian Gate in the Forbidden City. And other background buildings are like the memorial gateway, the screen wall and the stone lion. So the background building is very important in Chinese traditional construction, as it can show the building full of artistic.

The use of colors. The ancient craftsmen in China had the courage to use colors and was good at using them, which is closely connected with timber structural system of Chinese architectures. Owing to timber non-durable in use, in the early time, Chinese architects used the method that timber was painted coating and wood oil so that it could protect woods. In addition, it looked beautiful, and it was easy to use, which played an important role in combining appearance and usage. After practicing in a long time,

Chinese architects have accumulated plentiful experience in applying colors. For example, the ancient painters were good at contrast and harmony by bright colors in northern palace and bureaucratic buildings. The main part of the house, i. e. the part always shined sunshine, was normally painted in warm colors, especially vermilion. The shaded areas under the roof were painted cold colors such as blue and green. If so, it would emphasize warm sunshine and shady shadow to form a good-looking contrast. The part of vermilion door and window and blue-green roof always added gold thread and gold wire, and few red dots were decorated between blue and green colors, which made colorful pictures in the building more vivid and heighten decorative effect. Some important memorial architecture, such as the Forbidden City, the Temple of Heaven in Beijing, etc, would look more gorgeous under nice, clear and blue sky in North China. Plain if adding glazed tile with yellow, green or blue, and appending one or more layers of white marble stylobates and railings with snow-white. Certainly, to some extent, the forming of this color style is largely connected with natural environment in North, because in flat and broad North China Plain, the colors are monotonous and severe. In that natural environment, this bright color will bring vitality for architectures. Based on the same reason, in splendid and evergreen South, on one hand, the colors of architectures are limited by architectural hierarchy of feudal society. On the other hand, in South, trees are green all the year round and flowers are blooming throughout the growing seasons, in order to make the colors of architectures harmonious with surrounding environment in South, so buildings are painted in quiet and plain colors. Architects like to use white walls, gray tiles, black or dark green beam columns, which form a delicate, graceful and elegant style. This hue will produce a feeling of coolness in hot summer days in South, not like strong colors that are easy to make people restless. Therefore, the application of colors in ancient architectures makes a big difference according to different nationalities and areas.

Like the Chinese culture, the Chinese building is very famous in the world. It is not only history, but also the artistry. They Show the artistry from three different ways: the rich decorative roofs, the application of the background building and the use of colors. They are not just three independent parts, and there are very deep and complicated relationships between them.

Vocabulary

architecture *n.* 建筑学；建筑风格；建筑式样；架构
decorative *adj.* 装饰性的；装潢用的

anthology *n.* （诗、文、曲、画等的）选集
incise *vt.* 切；切割；雕刻
Meridian Gate *n.* 午门
timber *n.* 木材；木料
vermilion *n.* ［无化］朱砂；朱红色；*adj.* 朱红色的
glazed *adj.* 光滑的；像玻璃的；上过釉的；呆滞无神的；*v.* 上釉（glaze 的过去分词）
glazed tile 釉面砖
heighten *vt.* （使）加强；提高；增高；使更显著；*vi.* rise 升高；变强
stylobate *n.* 柱座（一列柱子下面的柱基）
monotonous *adj.* 单调乏味的，无抑扬顿挫的；无变化的

After You Read

Exercises

1. Answer the following questions.

(1) How many aspects do ancient Chinese people show the construction's artistries?
(2) Why is roof a very important part in Chinese architecture?
(3) What is the relationship between the main building and the back ground building?
(4) What do the building complexes include in China?
(5) What is the forming of the color style largely connected with?

2. Fill in the blanks with the words given below. Change the form where necessary. Each word can be used only once.

architect	harmonious	anthology	vermilion	increase
artistic	decorate	harmony	sculp	heighten

(1) It is an ____________ anthology that crackles with wit and wisdom.
(2) Painting, sculpture and ____________ architecture etc. are collectively called the "fine arts" or "plastic arts".
(3) In a ____________ decorative way, they were responding to the current sense of streamlining.
(4) I looked out again, he had held the ____________ vermilion oranges back.
(5) The move has ____________ heightened tension in the state.

(6) This style emphasizes the importance of team work, and creates ____________ harmony in a group by connecting people to each other.

(7) The management reacted to the demand of workers by ____________ increasing their wages since April.

(8) Various circumstances cooperated to make him a great ____________ artist.

(9) The same routine every week may become ____________ monotonous, so set some goals to help you stay focused.

(10) At that time, they made the comfortable incising on the ridge, and the tiles were made by the ____________ sculpture.

3. Decide whether the statements are true (T) or false (F) according to the passage.

(1) Construction principles of Chinese architecture have largely changed.

(2) We can find some poetries about roofs in "The Book of Songs".

(3) The relationship between main building and background building is like the relationship between flowers and green leaves.

(4) The application of colors in ancient architectures makes no difference according to different nationalities and areas.

(5) In order to make the colors of architectures harmonious with surrounding environment in South, so buildings are painted in quiet and plain colors.

4. Translation

(1) Chinese architecture is a style of architecture, which has formed many centuries in Eastern Asia.

(2) The Chinese ancient people made full use of the characteristic of the roofs.

(3) In the ancient Chinese palaces or temples, using background building to show the art and beauty are very common.

(4) The ancient craftsmen in China had the courage to use colors and was good at using them, which is close connected with timber structural system of Chinese architectures.

(5) After practicing in a long time, Chinese architects have accumulated plentiful experience in applying colors.

5. Pair work

Read the part "**The use of colors**" carefully and discuss the relationship between the application of colors and environment in ancient architectures. And then share your opinions with the class.

Read More

Extensive Reading

Text B

Totems in Chinese Traditional Architecture

The word totem means animal related to a group of people. A dragon and a phoenix, called Long and Feng in Chinese respectively, are totems of the Chinese people. Belief in the dragon, and drawings of the imaginary animal, can be traced back to primitive society when prehistoric tribes in China adopted the dragon among other totems as their symbol and guardian god.

The phoenix was commonly referred to as the "King of Birds", or a supernatural bird. It embodied the five virtues of benevolence, righteousness, propriety, wisdom, and sincerity.

The dragon and phoenix were used to decorate painted pottery and jade carvings in primitive society. The founding of the unified empire in the Qin Dynasty (221–206 BC) provided a base and motivation to develop the ancient Chinese palace architecture. Stone carvings, engraved brick, bronze ware and lacquer paintings were growing quickly. For the first time, the dragon and phoenix were heavily used on imperial architecture, especially on the imperial palaces' roofs, beams, pillars, and doors. Chinese architecture, as a kind of oriental art, has enveloped mystery with the decoration of the dragon and phoenix.

Chinese buildings, primarily timberwork, were formed into a system in the Qin and Han (206 BC – 220 AD) Dynasties. With the dragon totem, magnificent palatial architecture boarded this stage of history. From then on, the dragon and phoenix were status symbols of authority figures, treasure and emperors or the empresses. Decorations on the architecture of the Han Dynasty were single or and nose to tail dragon decorative patterns, which was basically Ying Loong with a long muzzle and neck.

With the collision of Buddhist art and traditional Chinese art, the dragon from the Wei (220–265) and Jin (265–581) Dynasties had ripples and a longer body and limbs. During the Sui (581–618) and Tang (618–907) Dynasties, dragons, with curly grass carving patterns, were always decorated on steles. In the Song (960–1279) and Yuan (1271–1368) periods, the shape of the dragon developed into a unique style as well as inheriting traditional techniques. In Ming (136 – 1644) and Qing (1644 – 1911) Dynasties, the dragon and phoenix were used to represent emperors and their consorts and were the main decorative patterns seen on various imperial structures. Palaces, columns, pathways and screen walls were all inscribed, carved or painted with their images.

The phoenix decorative pattern on architecture first appeared in the Qin and Han Dynasties. The pattern was discrepant in different regions but mostly had the head of a golden pheasant, the beak of a parrot, the body of a mandarin duck, the wings of a roe, the feathers of a peacock and the legs of a crane.

In the Wei and Jin Dynasties, craftsmen injected a new spirit of ideas into the image of the phoenix. The dragon-phoenix pattern absorbed the essence of foreign and Chinese traditional architectural art. The phoenix on the steles of the Sui and Tang Dynasties was more similar to raptors. In the Song and Yuan Dynasties, the phoenix was overwhelming and vigorous, which was full of romanticism. The dragon, phoenix and peony were common decoration themes in the Ming and Qing Dynasties. The phoenix was generally decorated with a ribbon and colorful feather, which is gloriously beautiful.

Chinese architecture is famous for timberwork, which is a platform for the dragon and phoenix totem. In the imperial palaces, the dragon and the phoenix were the principal motifs for decorative designs on the buildings. The daily clothing and articles for emperors and empresses were decorated with the dragon and phoenix. The throne hall was supported by columns entwined by gilded dragons, the central ramps on marble steps were paved with huge slabs carved in relief with the dragon and phoenix, and the screen walls display dragons in brilliant colors.

As a kind of unique building decoration style in China, the dragon and phoenix decorative patterns have been developed over thousands of years in the fertile land of the ancient Chinese civilization and showed social ideology and humanities in the spirit of Chinese ancestors. As Chinese style is prevalent today, the ancient Chinese dragon and phoenix totem shows the oriental fashion, and the culture of the dragon and phoenix have become an indispensable decorative element in Chinese architecture.

Vocabulary

benevolence *n.* 仁慈；善行

timberwork *n.* 木结构

motif *n.* 图形；图案

totem *n.*（尤指美洲土著的）图腾；图腾形象

embody *vt.* 体现，使具体化；具体表达

righteousness *n.* 正义；正直；公正；正当

discrepant *adj.* 有差异的；相差的；矛盾的

entwine *vt.* 缠住；盘绕；使缠绕；*vi.* 缠住；盘绕

indispensable *adj.* 不可或缺的；必不可少的；绝对必要的；责无旁贷的

collision *n.* 碰撞（或相撞）事故；（两人之间或对立意见、看法等之间的）冲突，抵触

ideology *n.* 思想（体系）；思想意识；意识形态；观念形态；思想意识；观念学

Exercises

1. Global reading

Decide whether the following statements are true（T）or false（F）.

（1）A dragon and a phoenix, called Long and Feng in Chinese respectively, are totems of the Chinese people.

（2）The dragon and phoenix were heavily used on imperial architecture, especially on the imperial palaces' roofs, beams, pillars, and doors after the Qin Dynasty for the first time.

（3）From the Qin and Han Dynasties on, the dragon and phoenix were status symbols of authority figures, treasure and emperors or the empresses.

（4）The shape of the dragon varies in different Dynasties.

（5）The culture of the dragon and phoenix have become an indispensable decorative element in Chinese architecture.

2. Questions for discussion

（1）Why are the dragon and phoenix used in Chinese Traditional Architecture?

（2）Where were the dragon and phoenix decorated in the imperial palaces?

（3）What totem cultures are there in the architecture of other countries?

3. Classroom activities

（1）Discuss the changes of architecture totems in different Dynasties.

（2）Imagine the development of totems in China's future architecture.

Text C
Features of Chinese Architecture

Chinese architecture refers to a style of architecture that has taken shape in East Asia over many centuries. The structural principles of Chinese architecture have remained largely unchanged, the main changes being only the decorative details. Since the Tang Dynasty, Chinese architecture has had a major influence on the architectural styles of Korea, Vietnam, and Japan.

The architecture of China is as old as Chinese civilization. From every source of information—literary, graphic, exemplary—there is strong evidence testifying to the fact that the Chinese have always enjoyed an indigenous system of construction that has retained its principal characteristics from prehistoric times to the present day. Over the vast area from Chinese Turkistan to Japan, from Manchuria to the northern half of French Indochina, the same system of construction is prevalent; and this was the area of Chinese cultural influence.

Throughout the 20th century, Western-trained Chinese architects have attempted to combine traditional Chinese designs into modern architecture (usually government), with only limited success. Moreover, the pressure for urban development throughout contemporary China required higher speed of construction and higher floor area ratio, which means that in the great cities the demand for traditional Chinese buildings, which are normally less than 3 levels, has declined in favor of modern architecture. However, the traditional skills of Chinese architecture, including major and minor carpentry, masonry, and stonemasonry, are still applied to the construction of vernacular architecture in the vast rural area in China.

Features of Chinese architecture falls into five categories.

Architectural bilateral symmetry

An important feature in Chinese architecture is its emphasis on articulation and bilateral symmetry, which signifies balance. Bilateral symmetry and the articulation of buildings are found everywhere in Chinese architecture, from palace complexes to humble farmhouses. When possible, plans for renovation and extension of a house will often try to maintain this symmetry provided that there is enough capital to do so. Secondary elements are positioned either side of main structures as two wings to maintain overall bilateral symmetry. The buildings are typically planned to contain an even number of columns in a structure to produce an odd number of bays. With the inclusion of a main door to a building in the centre bay, symmetry is maintained.

In contrast to the buildings, Chinese gardens are a notable exception which tend to be asymmetrical. The principle underlying the garden's composition is to create enduring flow.

Enclosure

Contemporary Western architectural practices typically involve surrounding a building by an open yard on the property. This contrasts with much of traditional Chinese architecture, which involves constructing buildings or building complexes that take up an entire property but enclose open spaces within itself. These enclosed spaces come in two forms: 1. Courtyard (院): The use of open courtyards is a common feature in many types of Chinese architectures. This is best exemplified in the Siheyuan, which consists of an empty space surrounded by buildings connected with one another either directly or through verandas. 2. "Sky well" (天井): Although large open courtyards are less commonly found in southern Chinese architecture, the concept of an "open space" surrounded by buildings, which is seen in northern courtyard complexes, can be seen in the southern building structure known as the "sky well". This structure is essentially a relatively enclosed courtyard formed from the intersections of closely spaced buildings and offer small opening to the sky through the roof space from the floor up.

These enclosures serve in temperature regulation and in venting the building complexes. Northern courtyards are typically open and facing the south to allow the maximum exposure of the building windows and walls to the sun while keeping the cold northern winds out. Southern sky wells are relatively small and serves to collect rain water from the roof tops. They perform the same duties as Roman impluvium while restricting the amount of sunlight that enters the building. Sky wells also serve as vents for rising hot air, which draws cool air from the lower stories of the house and allows for exchange of cool air with the outside.

Hierarchy

The projected hierarchy and importance and uses of buildings in traditional Chinese architecture are based on the strict placement of buildings in a property/complex. Buildings with doors facing the front of the property are considered more important than those facing the sides. Buildings facing away from the front of the property are the least important.

South-facing buildings in the rear and more private location of the property with higher exposure to sunlight are held in higher esteem and reserved for elder members of the family or ancestral plaques. Buildings facing east and west are generally for junior members of the family, while buildings near the front are typically for servants and hired help.

Front-facing buildings in the back of properties are used particularly for rooms of celebratory rites and for the placement of ancestral halls and plaques. In multiple courtyard complexes, central courtyards and their buildings are considered more important than peripheral ones, the latter typically being used as storage or servants' rooms or kitchens.

Horizontal emphasis

Classical Chinese buildings, especially those of the wealthy, are built with an emphasis on breadth and less on height, featuring an enclosed heavy platform and a large roof that floats over this base, with the vertical walls not well emphasized. This contrasts Western architecture, which tends to grow in height and depth. Chinese architecture stresses the visual impact of the width of the buildings.

The halls and palaces in the Forbidden City, for example, have rather low ceilings when compared to equivalent stately buildings in the West, but their external appearances suggest the all-embracing nature of imperial China. These ideas have found their way into modern Western architecture.

Cosmological concepts

Chinese architecture from early times used concepts from Chinese cosmology such as *feng shui* (geomancy) and Taoism to organize construction and layout from common residences to imperial and religious structures. This includes the use of:

Screen walls to face the main entrance of the house, which stems from the belief that evil things travel in straight lines.

Talismans and imagery of good fortune:

Door gods displayed on doorways to ward off evil and encourage the flow of good fortune.

Three anthropomorphic figures representing *Fu Lu Shou* (福禄寿) stars are prominently displayed, sometimes with the proclamation "the three stars are present" (三星在).

Animals and fruits that symbolize good fortune and prosperity, such as bats and pomegranates, respectively. The association is often done through rebuses.

Orienting the structure with its back to elevated landscape and ensuring that there is water in the front. Considerations are also made such that the generally windowless back of the structure faces the north, where the wind is coldest in the winter.

Ponds, pools, wells and other water sources are usually built into the structure.

The use of certain colors, numbers and the cardinal directions in traditional Chinese architecture reflected the belief in a type of immanence, where the nature of a thing could be wholly contained in its own form. Although the Western tradition gradually developed a body of architectural literature, little was written on the subject in China, and the earliest text, the Kaogongji, was never disputed. However, ideas about cosmic harmony and the order of the city were usually interpreted at their most basic level, so a reproduction of the "ideal" city never existed. Beijing as reconstructed throughout the 15th and 16th century remains one of the best examples of traditional Chinese town planning.

The architecture of China from the Neolithic (New Stone Age) culture to the 20th century, represents the most significant achievements of the world's longest continuous civilization. From large and extravagant temples to pleasant palaces, there are a lot to learn and see.

Vocabulary

indigenous *adj.* 本土的；土著的；国产的；固有的
contemporary *adj.* 当代的；同时代的；属于同一时期的
masonry *n.* 石工；石工行业；石造建筑
vernacular *adj.* 本国的；地方的；用本地语写成的
bilateral symmetry *n.* 两侧对称；左右对称
asymmetrical *adj.* ［数］非对称的（等于 asymmetric）；不均匀的；不匀称的
veranda *n.* 走廊，游廊；阳台
hierarchy *n.* 层级；等级制度
cosmological *adj.* 宇宙论的；宇宙哲学的
anthropomorphic *adj.* 拟人的，赋予人性的
extravagant *adj.* 奢侈的；浪费的；过度的；放纵的

Exercises

1. Global reading

Decide whether the following statements are true (T) or false (F).

(1) Since the Tang Dynasty, the architectural styles of Korea, Vietnam, and Japan

have been greatly influenced by Chinese architecture.

(2) Northern courtyards are typically open and facing the north to allow the maximum exposure of the building windows and walls to the sun while keeping the cold northern winds out.

(3) Buildings facing east and west are typically for servants and hired help, while buildings near the front are generally for junior members of the family.

(4) Chinese architecture lays stress on breadth and less on height while western architecture tends to grow in height and depth.

(5) The architecture of China from the Neolithic culture to the 20th century, represents the most significant achievements of the world's longest continuous civilization.

2. Questions for discussion

(1) What philosophical ideas does symmetry reflect in Chinese architecture?

(2) What is the difference between Chinese architecture and western architecture in horizontal emphasis?

(3) How do you interpret the significance of the wall in ancient Chinese architecture?

3. Classroom activities

(1) Discuss the differences between Chinese and western architectural concepts.

(2) Discuss the philosophical elements in Chinese architecture.

Text D
A Traditional *Siheyuan* in Beijing

The four buildings of a *Siheyuan* are normally positioned along the north-south and east west axis. The building positioned to the north and facing the south is considered the main house. The buildings adjoining the main house and facing east and west are called side houses. The northern, eastern and western buildings are connected by beautifully decorated pathways. These passages serve as shelters from the sunshine during the day and provide a cool lace to appreciate the view of the courtyard. The building that faces north is known as the opposite house. Behind the northern building there would often be a separate backside building, the only place where two story buildings are allowed to be constructed in the traditional *Siheyuan*.

The entrance gate, usually painted vermilion and with copper door knockers on it, is usually at the southeastern corner. Normally there is a screen wall inside the gate for privacy; superstition holds that it also protects the house from evil spirits. A pair of stone lions are often placed outside the gate. Some large *Siheyuan* compounds would have two or more layers of courtyards and even private gardens attached to them. That is a sign of wealth and status in ancient times.

The courtyard dwellings are built according to the traditional concepts of the five elements that are believed to compose the universe and the eight diagrams of divination. The gate is at the southeast corner which is the wind corner and the main house is built on the north side which is believed to belong to water, an element to prevent fire.

The layout of a simple courtyard represents traditional Chinese morality and Confucian ethics. In Beijing four buildings in a single courtyard receive different amounts of sunlight. The northern main building receives the most, thus serving as the living room and bedroom of the owner or head of the family. The eastern and western side buildings receive less and serve as the rooms for children or less important members of the family. The southern building receives the least sunlight and usually functions as a reception room and the servants dwelling, or a place where the family would gather to relax, eat or study. The backside building is for unmarried daughters and female servants: because unmarried girls were not allowed direct exposure to the public, they occupied the most secluded building in the *Siheyuan*.

A more detailed and further stratified Confucian order was followed in ancient China. The main house in the north was assigned to the eldest member of the family, i. e. the head of the family, usually grandparents. If the main house had enough rooms, a central room would serve as a shrine for ancestral worship. When the head of the household had concubines, the wife would reside in the room to the eastern end of the main house while the concubines would reside in the room to the western end of the main house. The eldest son of the family and his wife would live in the western side house while the younger son and his wife would reside in the eastern side house, he would take the opposite house in the south. Unmarried daughters would always stay in the backside building behind the main house.

When a funeral is held in a *Siheyuan*, the location of the casket depends on the status of the deceased, but all caskets are oriented so that the head of the deceased points south while the feet point north. If the deceased is the head of the household or his wife, then the casket would be on the center line in the main house. If the deceased was the concubine of the head of the household, her casket would remain in the main house, but could not be in the center. If the deceased is a younger male, then his casket is placed on the center line of the courtyard. If the deceased is a younger female, her casket is placed in the courtyard but cannot be on the center line.

Though from antiquity, a *Siheyuan* is a practically sound, engineered structure. Northwestern walls are usually higher than the other walls to protect the inside buildings from the harsh winds blowing across northern china in the winter. Eaves curve downward, so that rainwater will flow along the curve rather than dropping straight down. The rooftop is ridged to provide shade in the summer while retaining warmth in the winter.

A *Siheyuan* offers space, comfort, quiet and privacy. *Siheyuan* walls provide security as well as protection against dust and storms. With plants, rocks and flowers, the yard is also a garden and acts like an open-air living room. The veranda divides the courtyard into several big and small spaces that are not very distant from each other. Family members talk with each other here, creating a cordial atmosphere.

Vocabulary

adjoining *adj.* 邻接的；毗连的；*v.* 邻接（adjoin 的 ing 形式）
superstition *n.* 迷信
dwelling *n.* 住处；寓所；复数 dwellings；*v.* 居住（dwell 的现在分词）
divination *n.* 预测，占卜
Confucian ethics 儒家伦理
secluded *adj.* 隐蔽的；隐退的，隐居的
stratified *adj.* 分层的；形成阶层的；分为不同等级的
ancestral *adj.* 祖先的；祖传的
casket *n.* 棺材；骨灰盒；小箱；*vt.* 把……装进小箱；入殓
deceased *adj.* 已故的；*n.* 死者；[法] 被继承人；*vi.* 死亡（decease 的过去式）
eaves *n.* 屋檐；凸出的边缘

Exercises

1. Global reading

Decide whether the following statements are true (T) or false (F).

(1) The separate backside building behind the northern building is the only place

where two story buildings are allowed to be constructed in the traditional *Siheyuan*.

(2) The main house is built on the north side because it is believed to belong to water, and prevent fire.

(3) The southern building which receives the least sunlight just functions as a reception room and the servants dwelling.

(4) When the head of the household had concubines, they would reside in the room to the eastern end of the main house.

(5) If the deceased is the head of the household or his concubine, then the casket would be on the center line in the main house.

2. Questions for discussion

(1) What is the functions of the northern, eastern and western buildings which are connected by beautifully decorated pathways?

(2) What are the symbols of wealth and status in ancient times?

(3) Why is the backside building is for unmarried daughters and female servants?

3. Classroom activities

(1) Work in pairs and discuss the functions of a traditional *Siheyuan* in Beijing.

(2) Discuss what a more detailed and further stratified Confucian order was followed.

Suggestion for Further Reading

Guxi Pan. *A History of Chinese architecture*. China industrial architecture press, 2006.

Unit 5 Chinese Literature

After you have read more than ten thousand volumes, you will find it easy to write as if God were there helping you.

——Chinese Proverb

Unit Goals

- To get familiar with the four great classic novels of China.
- To get familiar with the five kinds of poetry.
- To learn about the life experience about Li Bai.
- To learn about the development of Chinese classical prose.
- To learn useful words and expressions that relate to Chinese literature and improve English languages skills.

Before You Read

1. Give the names of the following characters according to the pictures.

2. Discuss the following questions with your partner.

(1) What are the four great classic novels of China?

(2) Name a few well-known characters in the four great classic novels.

Intensive Reading

Text A
Four Great Classic Novels of China

Four long fictional novels are usually thought to be the best novels in Chinese literature. What all four have in common is that they were written in a spoken language of their times unlike most ancient literature that was written in the literary Classical Language. The four works were seminal for the development of Chinese societies in past eras. These four books are called the Four Great Classic Novels of China.

1. The Romance of the Three Kingdoms

The Romance of the Three Kingdoms is a semi-historical work said to be written by Luo Guanzhong. It is historical fiction about the lives and struggles of rulers and the wars at the end of the Han Dynasty and in the Three Kingdoms Period. The Han Dynasty had broken up into three big rival kingdoms. These kingdoms fought viciously. The big battles described are famous historical events. The novel describes the machinations, court intrigues, and the shifting alliances of the three kingdoms that emerged from the Han Empire.

2. Outlaws of the Marsh

Outlaws of the Marsh is about the lives and ideals of a group of characters who fought against the corrupt Song Dynasty. It is said it was written in vernacular language by Shi Nai An. The setting of the novel is during the Northern Song Dynasty era before the northern part of the Song Empire was overrun by a northern tribe and before the Mongols conquered the whole area. In the early tales or accounts, there were only about 40 outlaws, but the number in the band grew to more than 100. In the novel, the band fights the corrupt Song rulers.

3. Journey to the West

During the Tang Dynasty, a Buddhist named Xuanzang left Chang'an (Today's Xi'an) that was the capital of the Tang Empire to travel to India in order to collect scriptures and information. Chang'an was near the mouth of the Gansu Corridor that was a part of the Silk Road route in northwestern China.

He traveled through the Gansu Corridor and past the Flaming Mountains near Turpan. He was helped by Buddhists along the way, and spent about 13 years in India before he returned bearing Buddhist scriptures. This historic journey was retold in many legends and tales about an accompanying monkey. In the Ming Dynasty era (1368-1644), the fantastic tale, *Journey to the West*, was written, and it is regarded as one of the four best novels.

4. The Dream of the Red Chamber

The fourth major novel that made an impact on Chinese history and literature is *The Dream of the Red Chamber*. It was the last of the Four Classic Novels to be written. It is about the fortunes and lives of the people of two branches of a clan in the Qing Dynasty (1644-1911) era.

Vocabulary

seminal *adj.* （对以后的发展）影响深远的，有重大意义的
viciously *adv.* 暴力地；猛烈地；凶狠地
machination *n.* 阴谋；诡计
intrigue *n.* 阴谋诡计
alliance *n.* （国家、政党等的）结盟，联盟，同盟
outlaw *n.* 歹徒，罪犯；亡命之徒，逃犯；被剥夺法律保护者
marsh *n.* 湿地；沼泽；草本沼泽
Buddhist *n.* 佛教徒
vernacular *adj.* 方言；土语
clan *n.* 宗族，氏族，家族

After You Read

Exercises

1. Answer the following questions.

(1) What is it that all the four great classic novels have in common?

(2) What is *The Romance of the Three Kingdoms* about?

(3) What is the setting of *Outlaws of the Marsh*?

(4) Where is Chang An located during the Tang Dynasty?

(5) How many years did Xuanzang spent in India before he returned bearing Buddhist scriptures?

2. Fill in the blanks with the words given below. Change the form where necessary. Each word can be used only once.

vernacular	seminal	Buddhist	intrigue	viciously
alliance	machination	outlaw	marsh	clan

(1) ____________ is a religion which teaches that the way to end suffering is by overcoming your desires.

(2) What followed is a classic tale of power and ____________.

(3) There are a lot of frogs in the ____________.

(4) The snake raised its head as if to strike, but then it hissed ____________ .

(5) Through the ____________ of the evil Fairy, the level of the lake begins to subside.

(6) The film-maker is currently in post-production on Robin Hood, his retelling of the legend of Britain's most famous ____________, starring Russell Crowe.

(7) They were no longer a series of small bands but lived in a large community with more elaborate social organization, probably grouped into ____________ of people of common descent.

(8) The ____________ of these African tribes have never been written down.

(9) The Social Democrats are now in ____________ with the Greens.

(10) The start of the Gates foundation will absolutely be a ____________ moment.

3. Decide whether the statements are true (T) or false (F) according to the passage.

(1) *The Romance of the Three Kongdoms* is a semi-historical work said to be written by Shi Nai An.

(2) The Han Dynasty broke up into three big rival kingdoms.

(3) In the novel of *Outlaws of the Marsh*, the band fights the corrupt Song rulers.

(4) During the Tang Dynasty, a Buddhist named Xuanzang left Chang'an alone to travel to India in order to collect scriptures and information.

(5) *Journey to the West* was written in the Qing Dynasty.

4. Translation

(1) It is historical fiction about the lives and struggles of rulers and the wars at the end of the Han Dynasty and in the Three Kingdoms Period.

(2) The setting of the novel is during the Northern Song Dynasty era before the northern part of the Song Empire was overrun by a northern tribe and before the Mongols conquered the whole area.

(3) He traveled through the Gansu Corridor and past the Flaming Mountains near Turpan.

(4) During the Tang Dynasty, a Buddhist named Xuanzang left Chang'an (Today's Xi'an) that was the capital of the Tang Empire to travel to India in order to collect scriptures and information.

(5) It is about the fortunes and lives of the people of two branches of a clan in the Qing Dynasty (1644–1911) era.

5. Pair work

Think of a character in any of the four great classic novels and search for more information online. Share your information and comments about the character with the class.

Read More

Extensive Reading

Text B

Li Bai——A famous Romantic Poet

Li Bai's Poem

Li Bai is known as a famous Romantic Poet in ancient China. He was lived during the Tang Dynasty.

Along with writing romantic poems about women, he romanticized nature. Li Bai apparently led a wild life. He wrote about common things such as natural places and cities he saw, romance, war and death and things like this.

Along with having a wild life, writing poems and getting into trouble politically, he worked in the Hanlin Academy in Chang'an (now Xi'an), was a friend of the Emperor, and lived in exile.

Early Life

People are not sure where he was born. Some speculate that he was born in Central Asia. When he was young, he lived in Sichuan near Chengdu. There he liked to read and study ancient poetry and ancient texts such as the Dao De Jing that is the central text of Daoism. He was thought to be a genius, and he also practiced martial arts and killed people in duels.

Adult Life

In 725, when he was in his mid-twenties, Li Bai sailed from Sichuan down the Yangtze River all the way to Weiyang (Yangzhou) and Jinling (Nanjing). Along the way, he met and stayed with famous people and rulers. He then turned back to the southwest, met Xu Yushi, married the daughter of a former high official, and lived in Hubei. Then in 742, he went with a Daoist named Wu Yun to Chang'an.

He was introduced to the Emperor Xuanzong around 742. He became a friend of Emperor Xuanzong who appointed him to a post in the Hanlin Academy that was a group of scholars who advised the imperial court on affairs, and worked on academic matters.

But he was far from an academic in personality. He never passed the Confucian Imperial Examinations. He got into trouble with the emperor and his eunuch for writing romantic poems about them. He got drunk and got into trouble with them. Then, he left.

Then he wandered in the Tang Empire. He met Du Fu twice. They wrote poems about each other. Then he got into more political trouble. He was with Li Lin, Prince of Yung, who was then commander in chief of the Tang forces in central China.

In 757, he was in the fleet that was sailing against the imperial army. Perhaps he was merely visiting or perhaps he was an active in the rebellion. Li Lin was defeated, and he was banished to the southwest. Then he died five years later.

Comparison with Du Fu

Li Bai and Du Fu have a lot in common. Both worked as imperial court officials though neither of them passed the Imperial Examination, both lived in Sichuan, and both traveled.

However, they were also dissimilar. Du Fu was more of an academic Confucian. Li Bai was more of a Daoist. Du Fu wrote realistic poems and Li Bai wrote romantic poems. Du Fu wrote in a regulated poetic style called Shi, and Li Bai liked free-form poetry like a more ancient style. Both are said to have written more than a thousand poems, but people are not sure about how many of the poems ascribed to Li Bai were written by him.

They are considered China's best poets, and wrote about everyday topics like romance, war, death, natural beauty and ancient geographical places they saw. It may be that their poems are so popular partly because Chinese people like to read about ancient places. But unlike poets in later eras whose poems became more erudite and esoteric, they wrote about everyday things that people can appreciate.

Vocabulary

speculate *v.* 推测；猜测；推断
appoint *v.* 任命；委任
eunuch *n.* 阉人；太监；宦官
ascribe *v.* 认为……是（某人）所写
banish *v.* 放逐；流放；把（某人）驱逐出境
esoteric *adj.* 只有内行才懂的；难领略的
romanticize *v.* 使浪漫化；使传奇化；使更加富有吸引力
duel *n.* 决斗
imperial *adj.* 帝国的；皇帝的
rebellion *n.* 谋反；叛乱；反叛
erudite *adj.* 博学的；有学问的

Exercises

1. Global reading

Decide whether the following statements are true（T）or false（F）.

（1）Li Bai was lived during the Tang Dynasty.
（2）Li Bai wrote about common things such as natural places and cities he saw, romance, war and death.
（3）In 725, when he was in his thirties, Li Bai sailed from Sichuan down the Yangtze River all the way to Weiyang (Yangzhou) and Jinling (Nanjing).
（4）Li Bai passed the Confucian Imperial Examinations.
（5）Du Fu wrote romantic poems and Li Bai wrote realistic poems.

2. Questions for discussion

（1）Why did Li Bai get into trouble with the emperor and his eunuch?
（2）What are the similarities between Li Bai and Du Fu?
（3）What are the differences between Li Bai and Du Fu?

3. Classroom activities

（1）Search for representative poems written by Li Bai and share them with the class.

(2) Beside Li Bai and Du Fu, what other distinguished poets who were also lived in Tang Dynasty do you know? What are their representative poems?

Text C
Chinese Poetry

Poetry has been a favorite literary genre for thousands of years. Poetry isn't taken very seriously in the West, especially in the last two hundred years, but Chinese ancient poetry is still read and ancient Chinese poets are honored. The greatest poets are thought to have lived a thousand years ago or more during the Tang (618–907), Song (960–1279) and Han (206 BC–220 AD) Dynastic eras. Du Fu, Li Bai and Su Shi are considered among the best ancient poets, and there are five major kinds of major ancient poetic styles called *Shi*, *Ci*, *Ge*, *Qu* and *Fu*.

The very ancient poetry that was written a thousand or more years ago was simpler and about common things like love, romance and nature that people appreciate. Though much poetry was written in the eras following the Song Dynasty (960–1279), it is thought that the poets became increasingly erudite, academic and esoteric so that modern Chinese can't appreciate the style and meaning. Since the Chinese have a character-based writing system instead of an alphabetic system, though the languages have changed, modern Chinese can still read a lot of the ancient poetry. Since the pronunciation of words has changed a lot, often the rhymes or tonal rhythms are lost for poems that rhymed or had tonal patterns. But the meanings of the characters haven't changed much, though modern readers may interpret the words to mean something other than the ancient author intended. Nuances and connotations may be lost. Since old poems remain and modern Chinese can understand them to some extent, they are still appreciated.

Five Kinds of Poems

Shi

Shi poems are composed of couplets. They are poems of two more coupled lines. The two lines of a couplet usually rhyme and match rhythmically and complement each other tonally. Modern mandarin only has five tones, but ancient languages usually had more, so the tonal rhythms are generally lost.

Ci

Ci poetry can be described as poems that have patterns of syllables and tonal patterns. In making a *Ci* poetry, a poet chooses words that fit a specific pattern. These patterns may have once been part of a song. But the music has been lost. There are various patterns that provided affective settings for various effects or moods.

Ge

The word "*Ge*" means song. *Ge* poems are the words to a song that can be sung. There were folk songs as well as songs composed by the literate and educated composers.

Qu

When the Mongols conquered China and established the Yuan Dynasty (1279–1368), they brought with them their own style of music and forms of entertainment. They especially liked to watch shadow puppet theaters that were puppet plays of little manipulated figurines and puppets illuminated by a lamp so that the shadows fell against a screen. It is thought that the form of operatic drama of the Yuan Dynasty imitated their shadow play theaters. The style of music and song in the operas was called *Yuan Qu* or Mongol Music. The songs from the operas and popular songs were a poetic style called *Qu* that was also popular in later eras. The poetic style is freer of form.

Fu

A fifth major style of poetry is called "*Fu*". These are descriptive poems that contain both prose and couplets. These were popular about 1,500 years to 2,000 years ago. Often poets included rare or unusual written characters from preceding eras in their poems.

Vocabulary

genre *n.* 种类；类型
rhyme *n.* 押韵
connotation *n.* 含义；隐含意义
rhythmically *adv.* 有节奏地
puppet *n.* 木偶
couplet *n.* 对句（相连的两行长度相等的诗句）
nuance *n.* （意义、声音、颜色、感情等方面的）细微差别
alphabetic *adj.* 字母的
syllable *n.* 音节
manipulate *v.* 操纵；操作
illuminate *v.* 照亮
figurine *n.* 小雕像，小塑像

Exercises

1. Global reading

Decide whether the following statements are true (T) or false (F).

(1) The greatest poets are thought to have lived a thousand years ago or more during the Tang (618 – 907), Song (960 – 1279) and Han (206 BC – 220 AD)

Dynastic eras.

(2) There are five major kinds of major ancient poetic styles called *Shi*, *Ci*, *Ge*, *Qu* and *Fu*.

(3) The pronunciation of Chinese characters hasn't changed much along he history of development.

(4) *Shi* poems are poems of two more coupled lines.

(5) There are various patterns that provided affective settings for various effects or moods in *Ci* poetry.

2. Questions for discussion

(1) What's the difference between *Ci* and *Ge*?

(2) What did the Mongols bring with them when they conquered China and established the Yuan Dynasty?

(3) What are the characteristics of *Fu* poetry?

3. Classroom activities

(1) Work in pairs and discuss about the characteristics of the five kinds of poetry.

(2) Search online to find out some representative works of the five kinds of poetry and share the information with the class.

Text D
Chinese Classical Prose

Prose writing in ancient and pre-modern China differed from poetry in that it was less rigidly structured and wasn't like verses in a song or like one of the common styles of poetry. But compared to English prose, literary prose before the year 1900 was often much more formalized. Except for popular novels and theatrical plays, most of the literary prose works were written in the literary Classical Language. This Classical Language utilized the grammar and ancient characters of the Warring States Period (475–221 BC) and of the Han Dynasty era (206 BC –220 AD). Writers sought to imitate the examples of prose in ancient philosophical and religious books such as Mencius (孟子) and Zhuang Zi (庄子). These old texts that were thought to date from about 600 BC to 200 BC were thought to contain examples of careful and well-reasoned discourses and be examples of good organization and style. During the Han Dynasty era (206 BC–220 AD), a more formalized style of prose writing appeared that was called

Piantiwen（骈体文）or parallel prose style. But in the Tang and Song eras, people started to write in the less formal and more ancient style called *Guwen*（古文）of the Warring States era. So classical prose can be divided into three types called *Piantiwen* style, *Guwen* style, and the vernacular style used in operatic dramas and in the Four Classic Novels of Chinese literature.

For about 2,000 years after the Qin Dynasty era (221-206 BC), Chinese writers had a constraint that European writers generally didn't face after the Renaissance. Chinese writers generally needed to write in a common literary language that wasn't their native language or a vernacular language anywhere. The ancient languages of the Warring States Period were extinct. But writers had to maintain the grammar and the use of the vocabulary. In some ways, this is similar to how educated Europeans wrote in Latin until the Renaissance era.

During the Qin Dynasty (221-206 BC), the emperor ordered that all texts other than those of a philosophy called Legalism and some sciences that he favored be destroyed. There was a "Book Burning and the Burial of Scholars." They effectively destroyed several religions and philosophical schools and much ancient literature. During the Han era, people tried to reconstruct and preserve what was lost. What emerged as important were works attributed to Confucius, Mencius, Zhuang Zi, Lao Zi, and a few other philosophers. Mencius whose book was considered one of the major texts of Confucianism was said to have elegant diction, and Zhuang Zi whose text was one of the two pillars of the school of Daoism that emerged in the Han era showed how to use anecdotes and allegories effectively. Chinese writers tried to copy their styles. The example of the style from the pre-Qin era was said to be simple and direct.

In the Han era, a variant style was developed that was called *Piantiwen*（骈体文）. This style wasn't as clear or precise, but it was florid, ornate and rigid. The *Piantiwen* style was popular for several hundred years afterwards.

During the late Tang era (618-907), two prominent officials tried to reintroduce the earlier style called *Guwen*. Han Yu (768-824) and Liu Zongyuan tried to teach others to use *Guwen*. They are considered two of the great prose masters of the Tang and Song eras. But the Tang Dynasty fell and was replaced by the Song Dynasty (960-1279 AD). During the Song Dynasty, another literatus named Ouyang Xiu (1007-1072) helped to revive writing in the *Guwen* style. This neoclassical style dominated prose writing for the next 800 years. It was the writing system of rulers in the Ming (1368-1644) and Qing (1645-1912) eras.

In order to gain entrance into the bureaucracy during the Ming and Qing eras, candidates had to pass the imperial qualifying examination. The exam material was the 9 Classics of Neo-Confucianism as was codified in the Song era. The Four Books and Five Classics (四书五经) were basically memorized by those who did the best on the exams. These works contained the style of writing the literati wished to imitate.

After the fourteenth century, vernacular fiction became popular. This may be because the invention of printing allowed the works to be more widely published. In the Yuan (1279-1368), Ming and Qing eras, four novels were published that are considered the best in Chinese history. The four novels are often called the "Four Classics" in China. All four were written in a spoken language of their times unlike most ancient literature that was written in the literary Classical Language.

These four novels all have disputed authorship. They are: The Romance of the Three Kingdoms that is said to have been written by Luo Guan Zhong during the Yuan Dynasty (1279-1368); Outlaws of the Marsh that is said to be written by Shi Nai'an during the Yuan era; Journey to the West that is thought to have been published anonymously by Wu Cheng'en during the Ming Dynasty era (1368-1644); and The Dream of the Red Chamber was said to be written by Cao Xueqin (1715-1763) during the Qing Dynasty era (1644-1911). The writers wrote in different languages, but vernacular prose can be called the third type of classical prose writing.

Vocabulary

utilize *v.* 利用
diction *n.* 措辞；用语；用词
florid *adj.* 过分装饰的；过多修饰的
rigid *adj.* 死板的；僵硬的
neoclassical *adj.* 新古典主义的
allegory *n.* 寓言；讽喻；寓言体；讽喻法
vernacular *adj.* 地方性的
anecdote *n.* 逸事；趣闻
ornate *adj.* 华美的；富丽的；豪华的
literatus *n.* 学者
bureaucracy *n.* 官僚主义；官僚作风

Exercises

1. Global reading

Decide whether the following statements are true (T) or false (F).

(1) During the Qing Dynasty era, a more formalized style of prose writing appeared that was called *Piantiwen* or parallel prose style.

(2) In the Tang and Song eras, people started to write in the less formal and more ancient style called *Guwen* of the Warring States era.

(3) During the Han Dynasty, the emperor ordered that all texts other than those of a philosophy called Legalism and some sciences that he favored be destroyed.

(4) The ancient languages of the Warring States Period were extinct.

(5) During the late Tang era, three prominent officials tried to reintroduce the earlier style called *Guwen*.

2. Questions for discussion

(1) How did prose writing in ancient and pre-modern China differ from poetry?

(2) Why were religious books such as Mencius and Zhuang Zi thought to be examples of good organization and style?

(3) What are the characteristics of *Piantiwen*?

3. Classroom activities

(1) Work in pairs and discuss why the emperor ordered that all texts other than those of a philosophy called Legalism and some sciences that he favored be destroyed during the Qin Dynasty.

(2) Search online to find out the core thoughts and representative works of any literatus mentioned in the article.

Suggestion for Further Reading

Zhu Ziqing. *Spring*. Howard Goldblatt 译.

Unit 6 Chinese Operas

One minute's brilliant performance on the stage is attributed to ten years' practice under the stage.

——Chinese Proverb

Unit Goals

- To get familiar with the concept of traditional Chinese operas.
- To get familiar with different classical Chinese operas.
- To understand the contribution of the traditional Chinese operas.
- To learn useful words and expressions that relates to traditional Chinese operas and improve English languages skills.

Before You Read

1. Give the names of the following Chinese operas according to the pictures.

2. Look at the pictures above and then discuss the following questions with your partners.

(1) Briefly tell the origin of Chinese operas .

(2) Name a few well-known Chinese operas and share one story with your partner.

Intensive Reading

Text A
Chinese Operas

Chinese opera together with Greece tragic-comedy and Indian Sanskrit Opera are the three oldest dramatic art forms in the world. During the Tang Dynasty (618–907), the Emperor Taizong established an opera school with the poetic name Liyuan (Pear Garden). From that time on, performers of Chinese opera were referred to as'disciples of the pear garden'. Since the Yuan Dynasty (1271–1368) it has been encouraged by court officials and emperors and has become a traditional art form. During the Qing Dynasty (1645 – 1912), it became fashionable among ordinary people. Performances were watched in tearooms, restaurants, and even around makeshift stages.

It evolved from folk songs, dances, talking, antimasque, and especially distinctive dialectical music. Gradually it combined music, art and literature into one performance on the stage. Accompanied by traditional musical instruments like the Erhu, the gong, and the lute, actors present unique melodies—which may sound strange to foreigners—as well as dialogues which are beautifully written and of high literary value. These dialogs also promoted the development of distinct literary styles, such as Zaju in the Yuan Dynasty. For Chinese, especially older folks, to listen to this kind of opera is a real pleasure.

What appeals to foreigners most might be the different styles of facial make-up, which is one of the highlights and requires distinctive techniques of painting. Exaggerated designs are painted on each performer's face to symbolize a character's personality, role, and fate. This technique may have originated from ancient religions and dance. Audiences who are familiar with opera can know the story by observing the facial painting as well as the costumes. Generally, a red face represents loyalty and bravery; a black face, valor; yellow and white faces, duplicity; and golden and silver faces, mystery. Besides color, lines also function as symbols. For example, a figure can be painted either all white on his face, or just around the nose. The larger the white area painted, the more viperous the role.

Another technique that fascinates people is the marvelous acrobatics. Players can make fire spray out of their mouths when they act as spirits, or can gallop while squatting to act as a dwarf. This reflects a saying among actors: "One minute's performance on the stage takes ten years' practice behind the scenes."

Over the past 800 years, Chinese opera has evolved into many different regional varieties based on local traits and accents. Today, there are over 300 dazzling regional opera styles. Kun opera, which originated around Jiangsu Province, is a typical ancient opera style and features gentleness and clearness. This enabled it to be ranked among the World Oral and Intangible Heritages. Qinqiang opera from Shaanxi, known for its loudness and wildness, and Yu Opera, Yue Opera, and Huangmei Opera are all very enjoyable. Beijing Opera, the best-known Chinese opera style, was formed from the mingling of these regional styles.

Vocabulary

disciple *n.* 弟子；门徒；信徒
heritage *n.* 遗产；继承物
gallop *vt.* & *vi.* （使）疾驰
squat *vi.* 蹲坐；蹲
intangible *adj.* 难以明了的；无形的
duplicity *n.* 欺骗；口是心非；不诚实；二重性
dialectical *adj.* 辩证的；方言的
acrobatic *adj.* 杂技的
spray *vt.* & *vi.* 喷
valor *n.* 英勇；勇猛

After You Read

Exercises

1. Answer the following questions.

(1) What are the three oldest dramatic art forms in the world?
(2) When did Chinese operas become fashionable among ordinary people?
(3) Where did Chinese operas evolve from?
(4) How many techniques are there in Chinese operas? Please analyze them.

2. Fill in the blanks with the words given below. Change the form where necessary. Each word can be used only once.

dramatic	evolve	heritage	makeshift	melody
viperous	fascinate	trait	intangible	squat

(1) Many Victorians were shocked by the notion that Man had ____________ from lower forms of life.

(2) The beautiful ____________ is lingering in my mind.

(3) Our CEO talks and behaves without a ____________ of authority.

(4) A savage beast, the ____________ scourge of gods and humankind.

(5) The place continues to ____________ visitors, cloaked in its mystery.

(6) Good will is an ____________ asset.

(7) After a ____________ pause, the lawyer finished her summation.

(8) The old man ____________ down by the fire.

(9) The dining couch was a ____________, poor and patched but the best they had.

(10) These beautiful old palaces are part of our national ____________.

3. Decide whether the statements are true (T) or false (F) according to the passage.

(1) Since the Han Dynasty, Chinese operas has become a traditional art form.

(2) Chinese operas were evolved from folk songs, dances, talking, antimasque, and especially distinctive dialectical music.

(3) During the Qing Dynasty, Chinese operas became fashionable among ordinary people.

(4) Marvelous acrobatics is one of the techniques that Chinese operas fascinates people.

(5) Beijing Opera was formed from the mingling of the regional styles.

4. Translation

(1) Chinese opera together with Greece tragic-comedy and Indian Sanskrit Opera are the three oldest dramatic art forms in the world.

(2) Since the Yuan Dynasty (1271–1368) it has been encouraged by court officials and emperors and has become a traditional art form.

(3) Accompanied by traditional musical instruments like the Erhu, the gong, and the lute, actors present unique melodies—which may sound strange to foreigners—as well as dialogues which are beautifully written and of high literary value.

(4) Players can make fire spray out of their mouths when they act as spirits, or can gallop while squatting to act as a dwarf.

(5) Over the past 800 years, Chinese opera has evolved into many different regional varieties based on local traits and accents.

5. Pair work

Watch a well-known Chinese opera and introduce it to your partner in English. And then share the best story and comments with the class.

Read More

Extensive Reading

Text B
The Four Most Popular Chinese Operas

Chinese opera is an ancient art form with enduring charms. There are more than 360 types of Chinese operas, with Beijing Opera, Huangmei Opera, Yue Opera and Yu Opera considered the four most famous.

1. Beijing Opera

The Beijing Opera is considered the quintessential Chinese performance art. It originated in Beijing but has spread all around China to become a symbol of Chinese culture. Combining singing, dancing, dialogue and martial arts, it has five main types of characters: Sheng, Dan, Jing, Mo, Chou. These refer to male characters, female characters, forceful characters, middle-aged male characters and comedic figures respectively. Because the Beijing Opera was originally a feature of the imperial palace, it had stricter requirements for the performance, costumes, makeup and songs.

2. Yu Opera

The Yu Opera originated in Henan Province and is the most widely performed type of local opera in China, having 167 professional troupes around the country as of 2006. The Yu Opera is characterized by its sonorous tone, cadence and intonation. It uses a wide variety of traditional Chinese instruments including fifes, silk strings and the Suona, which resembles a small trumpet. The stage display is simple and all the performers usually wear thick makeup.

3. Yue Opera

The Yue Opera, from the southern costal areas of China, is lyrical and centers around singing. Usual themes include gifted scholars and beautiful ladies, and the love story *The Butterfly Lovers* is well-known example. During its development, the Yue Opera has undergone a historical change from having mainly male performers to mostly female performers, making it a distinctive feature of Yue Opera that even its male roles are performed by actresses.

4. Huangmei Opera

The Huangmei Opera originates from Huangmei, Hubei, and is a very lively form of opera that tells the life stories of ordinary people. Legend says that because Huangmei is located on the northern bank of the Yangtze River, it was frequently struck by natural disasters, especially floods. Its residents were forced to learn Huangmei Opera to beg in other places, which promoted the spread of this folk art. The most famous piece of Huangmei Opera is *The Goddess Marriage*.

Vocabulary

quintessential *adj.* 典型的，完美的；精髓的
martial arts *n.* 武术
respectively *adv.* 分别地；各自地，独自地
imperial *adj.* 帝国的；皇帝的；至高无上的；威严的
costume *n.* 服装，装束；戏装，剧装
troupe *n.* 剧团；一班；一团
sonorous *adj.* 响亮的；作响的；能发出响亮声音的
cadence *n.* 节奏；韵律；抑扬顿挫
intonation *n.* 声调，语调；语音的抑扬
distinctive *adj.* 独特的，有特色的；与众不同的

Exercises

1. Global reading

Decide whether the following statements are true (T) or false (F).

(1) There are only 360 types of Chinese operas, with Beijing Opera, Huangmei Opera, Yue Opera and Yu Opera considered the four most famous.

(2) Chinese operas originated in Beijing but has spread all around China to become a symbol of Chinese culture.

(3) The Yue Opera, from the northern costal areas of China, is lyrical and centers around singing.

(4) The most famous piece of Huangmei Opera is The Butterfly Lovers.

(5) During its development, the Yue Opera has undergone a historical change from having mainly male performers to mostly female performers.

2. Questions for discussion

(1) To the passage, how many main types of characters in Beijing Opera? What are they?

(2) Why does Beijing Opera have a stricter requirements for the performance, costumes, makeup and songs?

(3) What does legend say about Huangmei Opera?

3. Classroom activities

Beside these four most famous Chinese operas, what other operas do you know? Introduce them to your classmates.

Text C
Beijing Opera

Beijing Opera or Peking Opera is a kind of Chinese opera and has a 200-year-long history. Its main melodies originated from Xipi and Erhuang in Anhui and Hubei respectively, it is believed that Beijing Opera gradually came into being after 1790 when the famous four Anhui opera troupes came to Beijing. Beijing Opera underwent fast development during the reign of Emperor Qianlong and the notorious Empress Dowager Cixi under the imperial patron, eventually becoming more accessible to the common people.

There are four roles in Beijing Opera—*Sheng* (a male role, usually a leading one), *Dan* (female roles), *Jing* (painted-face roles) and *Chou* (Clown role). These roles have the natural features of age and sex, as well as social status, and are artificially exaggerated by makeup, costume and gestures. All but the second portray a male or masculine character. Until recently, even that of the female or feminine character was played by a male actor.

Costumes are an integral part of the Beijing Opera performance. That are called

Xingtou or *Xifu* in Chinese. In the early days, opera costumes were mainly made of wool or coarse cloth; later, satin, crepe and silk were used, decorated with various meticulously embroidered patterns. The making of opera costumes is a special and unique stagecraft. The costume box first appeared in the Ming Dynasty, and was greatly improved in the Qing Dynasty.

Beijing Opera's Performers have two main methods of makeup: masks and facial painting. The frequent on-stage change of masks, without the audience noticing, is a special technique, known as changing faces. Opera facial painting falls into four categories-personality makeup (facial designs, painted faces or *Lian Pu*), decorative makeup (decorated faces), mood makeup (changing facial designs), and pictographic makeup (animal-like facial designs).

Art of illusion and imagination is one of Beijing Opera's most important features, expressed through exaggeration and concentration. Background and props are kept to a minimum and remain simple, usually a table and two chairs in front of a big curtain. Performers use gesture and body language to represent actions such as opening or closing the door, going up or down a building or a mountain, and embarking, disembarking or traveling by boat. A decorated whip represents horse, a paddle a boat and two pennants embroidered with wheels a carriage. When the actor walks in a circle, it means that he is in a long journey. Four generals and four soldiers represent an army. Two actors can portray groping and fighting dark through dance and acrobatics on a brightly lit stage. By such techniques, Beijing Opera has made it possible to transform a small stage into the whole universe.

In ancient times, Beijing Opera was performed mostly on stage in the open air, teahouses or temple courtyards. The most famous stage for the imperial of Beijing Opera—Deheyuan, it's built in the late 19th Century at the command of the Empress Dowager Cixi inside the Summer Palace in Beijing. Nowadays, the best well—preserved wooden opera theatres are Huguang Guild Hall, Lao She Teahouse and Zhengyici Theatre, there are the home to some of the best Beijing Opera actors and opens its doors to Beijing Opera lovers, locals and tourists to share an interesting and unique opera experience.

Vocabulary

troupe *n.* 剧团；一班；一团
reign *n.* 君主统治时期；任期
notorious *adj.* 声名狼藉的，臭名昭著的
imperial *adj.* 帝国的；皇帝的；至高无上的；威严的

patron *n.* 赞助人；保护人；主顾
accessible *adj.* 易接近的；可进入的；可理解的
exaggerate *v.* 使扩大；使增大
masculine *adj.* 男性的；阳性的；男子气概的
integral *adj.* 积分的；完整的，整体的；构成整体所必须的
meticulously *adv.* 细致地；一丝不苟地；拘泥地
embroider *v.* 刺绣；装饰；镶边
pictographic *adj.* 象形文字的，绘画文字的
embark *v.* 上船（或飞机）；（使）上船（或登记）；从事

Exercises

1. Global reading

Decide whether the following statements are true（T）or false（F）.

(1) It is believed that Beijing Opera gradually came into being after 1790 when the famous four Anhui opera troupes came to Beijing.

(2) In the early days, opera costumes were mainly made of wool or coarse cloth and decorated with various meticulously embroidered patterns.

(3) Art of illusion and imagination is not one of Beijing Opera's most important features, expressed through exaggeration and concentration.

(4) In ancient times, Beijing Opera was performed only on stage in the open air, teahouses or temple courtyards.

(5) Beijing Opera's Performers have two main methods of makeup: masks and facial painting.

2. Questions for discussion

(1) What are the four roles in Beijing Opera? And state the features of these roles.

(2) What are the four categories of Beijing Opera's facial painting?

(3) What is the most important feature of Beijing Opera? Use your own words to introduce its feature briefly.

3. Classroom activities

(1) Wok in pairs and discuss how do you understand "Art of illusion and imagination is one of Beijing Opera's most important features, expressed

through exaggeration and concentration"?

(2) Can you give an example of a famous artist of Beijing Opera?

Text D
Kunqu Opera

Kunqu Opera is one of the oldest forms of opera still existing in China, with its origins dating back to the Yuan Dynasty (1271 - 1368). It has distinguished itself by the virtuosity of its rhythmic patterns and has exerted a dominant influence on all the more recent forms of opera in China, including the Sichuan and Beijing operas.

In 2001, UNESCO (United Nations Educational, Cultural and Scientific Organization) proclaimed Kunqu Opera as a masterpiece of the Oral and Intangible Heritage of humanity (a UNESCO program that ensures that the best of every country's traditions is preserved and developed as well as made known to the outside world).

Description

Kunqu Opera, also called *Kunshanqiang* (昆山腔), is said to be the mother of all Chinese operas. Its beginnings can be traced to the late Yuan Dynasty, some 600 years ago, in the lower Yangtze Valley (长江流域). Among the earliest genres of drama, the traditional performing art was named for its birthplace, Kunshan, near the city of Suzhou in today's Jiangsu Province of East China.

The development of Kunqu Opera music went through several stages. In the early days, the songs were composed of long and short lines. The singer sang solo, and the orchestra came in at the end of each line. In the course, only percussion instruments were used.

In the Ming Dynasty (1368-1644), reformed by Wei Liangfu (魏良辅) during the reign of Emperor Jiajing, Kunqu Opera became mild, smooth and graceful. The performers attached great importance to clear recitation, correct singing, and pure tunes. Meanwhile, the composers wrote the musical scores after working out the tunes, and the songs were written in seven-character or ten-character lines. Moreover, three types of musical instruments (stringed instruments, bamboo flutes, and drums and clappers) formed the accompaniment. In addition, the jing and chou roles were no longer those exclusively portraying foolish, awkward, or stingy people.

Kunqu Opera is acknowledged as an elegant opera in terms of music, recitation, and the performers' movement. It is foremost acclaimed as "watermill song" because of its soft arias and the graceful movement of its performers. Carrying forward the tradition of ancient poetry and common speech, the art is also of very high literary value.

Kunqu has its own distinctive tunes. The orchestra consists of traditional instruments including the dizi, a horizontal bamboo flute which plays the lead part; the xiao, a vertical bamboo flute; the sheng, a mouth organ; and the pipa, a plucked string instrument with a fretted finger board. Many Chinese local operas are greatly influenced by its tunes and acting style.

Risk of Disappearance

Kunqu Opera, acknowledged as an elite opera, has suffered some of a decline since the eighteenth century because it requires a high level of technical knowledge from the audience. Today, it is facing competition from mass culture and a lack of interest amongst the young. Of the 400 arias regularly sung in opera performances in the mid-20th century, only a few dozen continue to be performed.

The Rebirth of the Kunqu Opera

A young girl appears as soon as the first notes of music are heard. Draped in a richly embroidered costume, she performs graceful hand movements. The elegance of her gestures is enhanced by her long silk sleeves. Accompanied by a flute, she begins to sing and the audience holds its breath.

The scene is an excerpt from The Peony Pavilion (游园惊梦), written by Tang Xianzu (汤显祖) who lived in 16th century and is now known as "China's Shakespeare". Kunqu Opera is now becoming the object of renewed interest although it has long being threatened with extinction. Since 2001 when Kunqu Opera was proclaimed as a Masterpiece of the Oral and Intangible Heritage, the traditional performing art has experienced a rebirth in the past few years. Four classical plays, including The Peony Pavilion, have been restored and updated.

The Peony Pavilion tells the tragic tale of Du Liniang (杜丽娘), who dreams during a walk in the park that she meets and falls in love with a young man. Unable to live her dream in reality, she falls mortally ill and, as she is dying, asks to be buried in the garden where she met her beloved. Later, Liu Mengmei, a student on his way to the capital, passes in front of Du Liniang's house and asks to spend the night there. As he sleeps, he dreams about the young girl. Revealing to him that he is the one her heart desires, she asks him to open her coffin. Liu Mengmei does so and Du Liniang comes back to life.

Since 2004, this updated version of the play, produced by Bai Xianyong (白先勇), one of China's best-known contemporary authors, has been staged in a dozen universities in China. Teachers and students can buy tickets for as little as 10 yuan (US$1.23). Each time the performance attracts a large audience who praises the opera as being very sweet, graceful, and profoundly touching.

Action Plan

The Opera Research Institute of the Chinese Academy of Arts maintains a rich collection of written and audiovisual resources and conducts research into a wide range of areas.

The State funds seven permanent theaters, which specialize in Kunqu Opera and encompass a total of 500 practitioners. Two of these theaters also offer classes. The action plan aims to publish a complete edition of the texts of Kunqu Operas since the Ming era, to produce an archive of the expertise of elderly actors through video recordings and to revive those plays which have not been performed for a considerable time.

Furthermore, the actors training program needs to be strengthened to allow an intake of around 10 students per year and to be widened to incorporate training for technical experts, researchers, and directors.

Vocabulary

stingy *adj.* 吝啬的；小气的
fret *n.* ［音］音品；音柱
embroider *v.* 刺绣；镶边；装饰
horizontal *adj.* 水平的；横的
intake *n.* 吸入；招收；入口；通风口
elite *adj.* 精英的；优秀的
dominant *adj.* 主要的；占优势的；显性的
encompass *vt.* 围绕；包围；包括；完成
proclaim *vt.* 正式宣布；声明；表明；赞扬
percussion *n.* 碰撞；打击乐器；［医］叩诊
reign *n.* 君主统治；在位期 *v.* 统治；支配
exclusively *adv.* 专门地；排他地；独占地；仅仅；只
distinguished *adj.* 卓越的，著名的；高贵的，受尊重的
virtuosity *n.* 精湛技巧；对艺术品的欣赏或爱好；艺术爱好者

Exercises

1. Global reading

Decide whether the following statements are true（T）or false（F）.

（1）Kunqu Opera is one of the oldest forms of opera still existing in China, with its origins dating back to the Song Dynasty.

(2) In 2001, UNESCO (United Nations Educational, Cultural and Scientific Organization) proclaimed Kunqu Opera as a masterpiece of the Oral and Intangible Heritage of humanity.

(3) In the early days, the songs of Kunqu Opera were composed of long and short lines.

(4) The tunes and acting style of Kunqu Opera are greatly influenced by many Chinese local operas.

(5) Of the 400 arias regularly sung in opera performances in the mid-20th century, only a few dozen continue to be performed.

2. Questions for discussion

(1) When did UNESCO proclaim Kunqu Opera as a masterpiece of the Oral and Intangible Heritage of humanity?

(2) Acknowledged as an elite opera, why did Kunqu Opera have suffered some of a decline since the eighteenth century?

(3) What is the action plan of the Opera Research Institute of the Chinese Academy of Arts?

3. Classroom activities

Wok in pairs and discuss the famous scenes of Kunqu Operas, then choose the one you like best and share its excellent part with your classmates.

Suggestion for Further Reading

李颖洁，曹丹，梁怡雯，等. *The Effect of Beijing Opera on Emotional Processing* [J]. Advances in Psychology. 2012, 2 (5): 236~242.

Unit 7 Traditional Chinese Medicine

Unit Goals

- To get familiar with the concept of Traditional Chinese medicine.
- To get familiar with the Four Great Classics.
- To understand the contribution of the Traditional Chinese medicine.
- To learn useful words and expressions that relates to traditional chinese medicine and improve English languages skills.

Before You Read

1. Give the names of the following medical scientists according to the pictures.

2. Look at the pictures above and then discuss the following questions with your partners.

(1) Briefly tell the origin of traditional Chinese Medicine (TCM).

(2) Name a few well-known TCM physicians/surgeons and share one story with your partner.

Intensive Reading

Text A
The History of Traditional Chinese Medicine

Traditional Chinese medicine (TCM), with a history of thousands of years, unique and integrated theoretical system, rich practical experience and good clinical effect, has been making great contribution to Chinese people's health care and the development of Chinese nation. It is a summary of the Chinese people's experience in their struggle against diseases. Over the past few decades it has been attracting increasing attention from all over the world.

The formation of TCM theoretical system can be traced back to the period of the Warring States and the Qin and Han Dynasties. During the long course of TCM development, the ancient medical experts took ancient Chinese philosophical thinking as the guide constantly absorbing knowledge from ancient natural and social sciences. The compilation of *Huangdi Neijing* (*Huangdi's Canon of Medicine*), *Nan Jing* (Classic of Difficulties), *Shanghan Zabing Lun* (*Treatise on Cold Damageand Miscellaneous Diseases*), and *Shennong Bencao Jing* (*Shennong's Classic of Materia Medica*), known in TCM as the Four Great Classics, is the symbol of the primary formation of the theoretical system of TCM.

Huangdi Neijing, as the earliest and greatest medical classic extant in China, was completed by many medical experts in history. And so important is it considered that even at present, after thousands of years, it is still regarded as the most authoritative one in TCM. The content of *Huangdi Neijing* covers the following aspects: the correspondence between man and nature, physiology and pathology of the human body as well as diagnosis, treatment and prevention of diseases. By applying the theories of yin-yang and the five elements, it has developed the therapeutic principles based on syndrome differentiation, seasonal changes, geographical localities and individual constitution.

Nan Jing was written approximately before the Han Dynasty and, according to legend, by Qin Yueren, also known as Bian Que. It deals mainly with the basic theory of TCM, including the knowledge of physiology, pathology, diagnostics and therapeutics. It has supplemented what was unaddressed in *Huangdi Neijing* in many respects, especially in pulse lore.

Shennong Bencao Jing, the earliest book on material medica in China, appeared approximately in the Han Dynasty with its authorship unknown. In this classic, 365 kinds of medicine are recorded, among which 252 are herbs, 67 are animal parts and 46 are mineral products. They are divided into three grades according to their properties and effects.

Shanghan Zabing Lun was written by Zhang Zhongjing at the end of the Eastern Han Dynasty. In this book the rich experience on prevention and treatment of diseases before the Eastern Han Dynasty was summed up, diagnosis and treatment of cold and miscellaneous diseases were dealt with respectively. This book symbolizes the establishment of treatment based on syndrome differentiation in TCM.

Vocabulary

physiology *n.* 生理学
therapeutic *adj.* 治疗学
diagnostics *n.* 诊断学
miscellaneous *adj.* 各式各样的
compilation *n.* 收集（资料）并编辑（成书、表、报告等）
authoritative *adj.* 有权利的；有权威的；可相信的；可靠的
pathology *n.* 病理学
syndrome *n.* 综合病症；综合症状
lore *n.* 学问，知识
clinical *adj.* 临床的；有关临床的

After You Read

Exercises

1. Answer the following questions.

(1) What time did the TCM theoretical system primarily?
(2) Which one of the four great classics in TCM whose authorship is definitely known?
(3) What are the theoretical and clinical characteristics of TCM?
(4) What is the contribution of *Nan Jing*?
(5) Which Classic divided into three grades according to their properties and effects?

2. Fill in the blanks with the words given below. Change the form where necessary. Each word can be used only once.

compilation	physiology	pathology	diagnostics	clinical
herb	diagnose	miscellaneous	syndrome	therapeutic

(1) In 1984, he was ____________ with diabetes, a medical condition caused by a lack of insulin, which makes the patients produce a lot of urine and feel thirsty.

(2) Yoga is a ____________ physical exercises that focuses on breathing and relaxation.

(3) The medicine chemically affects your ____________.

(4) This ____________ was first issued on vinyl in 1990.

(5) The eighteenth century saw the development of modern ____________ and experimental surgery.

(6) Lemon juice can help to prevent economy-class ____________ by improving blood circulation.

(7) The ____________ has been used for centuries to tablet.

(8) They eat a lot of meats and dairy foods, along with a lot of ____________ items .

(9) She was diagnosed as being ____________ depressed.

(10) An intelligent computer will be an indispensable ____________ tool for doctors.

3. Decide whether the statements are true (T) or false (F) according to the passage.

(1) TCM theoretical system can be traced back to Tang Dynasty.

(2) *Shennong Bencao Jing* has developed the therapeutic principles based on syndrome differentiation, seasonal changes, geographical localities and individual constitution.

(3) *Nan Jing* was written by Bian Que, approximately before the Han Dynasty.

(4) *Shennong Bencao Jing* was not the earliest book on material medica in China.

(5) *Shanghan Zabing Lun* symbolizes the establishment of treatment based on syndrome differentiation in TCM.

4. Translation

(1) Traditional Chinese medicine, with a history of thousands of years, unique and

integrated theoretical system, rich experience and good effect, has been making great contributions to Chinese people's health and the development of Chinese nation.

(2) The formation of TCM theoretical system can be traced back to the period of the Warring States and the Qin and Han Dynasties.

(3) It has supplemented what was unaddressed in *Huangdi Neijing* in many respects, especially in pulse lore.

(4) *Huangdi Neijing*, as the earliest and greatest medical classic extant in china, was completed by many medical experts in history.

(5) In this book the rich experience on prevention and treatment of diseases before the Eastern Han Dynasty was summed up, diagnosis and treatment of cold and miscellaneous diseases were dealt with respectively.

5. Pair work

Read a well-known TCM physicians or surgeon and tell your partner about the story in English. And then Share the best story and comments with the class.

Read More

Extensive Reading

Text B

Traditional Chinese Medicine: An Introduction

1. Traditional Chinese medicine (TCM) originated in ancient China and has evolved over thousands of years . TCM practitioners use herbs acupuncture, and other methods to treat a wide range of conditions. In the United States, TCM is considered part of complementary and alternative medicine (CAM). This following fact provides a general overview of TCM and suggests sources for additional information.

Background

2. Traditional Chinese medicine, which encompasses many different practices, is rooted in the ancient philosophy of Taoism and dates back more than 5,000 years. Today, TCM is practiced side by side with Western medicine in many of China's hospitals and clinics.

3. TCM is widely used in the United States. Although the exact number of people who use TCM in the United States is unknown, it was estimated in 1997 that some 10,000 practitioners served more than 1 million patients each year. According to the 2007

National Health Interview Survey, which included questions on the use of various CAM therapies, an estimated 3.1 million U.S. adults had used acupuncture in the previous year. In addition, according to this same survey, approximately 17 percent of adults use natural products, including herbs, making it the most commonly used therapy. In another survey, more than one-third of the patients at six large acupuncture clinics said they also received Chinese herbal treatments at the clinics.

Underlying Concepts

4. Underlying the practice of TCM is a unique view of the world and the human body that is different from Western medicine concepts. This view is based on the ancient Chinese perception of humans as microcosms of the larger, surrounding universe—interconnected with nature and subject to its forces. The human body is regarded as an organic entity in which the various organs, tissues, and other parts have distinct functions but are all interdependent. In this view, health and disease relate to balance of the functions.

5. The theoretical framework of TCM has a number of key components:

Yin-Yang theory—the concept of two opposing, yet complementary, forces that shape the world and all life—is central to TCM.

In the TCM view, a vital energy or life force called *qi* circulates in the body through a system of pathways called meridians. Health is an ongoing process of maintaining balance and harmony in the circulation of *qi*.

The TCM approach uses eight principles to analyze symptoms and categorize conditions: cold/heat, interior/exterior, excess/deficiency and *Yin/Yang* (the chief principles). TCM also uses the theory of five elements—fire, earth, metal, water, and wood—to explain how the body works; these elements correspond to particular organs and tissues in the body. These concepts are documented in the *Huangdi Neijing* (*Inner Canon of the Yellow Emperor*), the classic Chinese medicine text.

Treatment

6. TCM emphasizes individualized treatment. Practitioners traditionally used four methods to evaluate a patient's condition: observing (especially the tongue), hearing/smelling, asking/interviewing, and touching/palpating (especially the pulse).

7. TCM practitioners use a variety of therapies in an effort to promote health and treat disease. The most commonly used are Chinese herbal medicine and acupuncture.

- Chinese herbal medicine. The *Chinese Materia Medica* (a pharmacological reference book used by TCM practitioners) contains hundreds of medicinal substances-primarily plants, but also some minerals and animal products-classified by their perceived action in the body. Different parts of plants such as the leaves, roots, stems, flowers, and seeds are used. Usually, herbs are combined in formulas and given as teas, capsules, tinctures, or powders.

- Acupuncture. By stimulating specific points on the body, most often by inserting thin metal needles through the skin, practitioners seek to remove blockages in the flow of *qi*.

Vocabulary

acupuncture *n.* 针刺疗法
microcosm *n.* 缩影；具体而微者
meridian *n.* 子午线，经线，顶点
palpate *v.* （医）触诊，触摸检查
tincture *n.* 酊；酊剂
practitioner *n.* （尤指医学或法律界的）从业者
circulate *v.* （液体或气体）环流，循环，流通
therapy *n.* 治疗；疗法
deficiency *n.* 缺乏；缺少；不足
capsule *n.* （装药物的）胶囊
powder *n.* 粉末；洗面
blockage *n.* 造成堵塞的东西；阻塞物

Exercises

1. Global reading

Decide whether the following statements are true（T） or false（F）.

（1） In the United States, TCM is not considered part of complementary and alternative medicine.（CAM）

（2） Traditional Chinese medicine is rooted in the ancient philosophy of Taoism and dates back more than 6,000 years.

（3） Many Americans also received Chinese herbal treatments at the clinics.

（4） Health is a continual process of maintaining balance and harmony in the circulation of *qi*.

（5） Some parts of plants such as the roots, seeds are not used in the Chinese herbal medicine.

2. Questions for discussion

（1） According to the 2007 National Health Interview Survey, what is the situation of the use of CAM therapy in the USA?

(2) Why is TCM said to have a unique view of the world and the human body?
(3) What are the key components of the theoretical framework of TCM?

3. Classroom activities

(1) Beside herbal remedies and acupuncture, what other practices are commonly used by TCM practitioners?
(2) What are the four methods traditionally used by TCM practitioners to evaluate a patient's condition?

Text C
Application of *Yin-Yang* to Medicine

The opposition of *yin-yang* is reflected in medicine in the opposing *yin-yang* structure of the human body, the opposing *yin-yang* character of the organs and, most of all, the opposing symptomatology of *yin* and *yang*. No matter how complicated, all symptoms and signs in Chinese medicine can be reduced to their elemental, basic character of *yin* or *yang*. In order to interpret the character of the clinical manifestations in terms of *yin-yang* we can refer to certain basic qualities that will guide us in clinical practice.

For example, fire-water is one of the fire fundamental dualities of *yin-yang* in Chinese medicine. Although these terms derive from the five-element theory, there is an interaction between that and the theory of *yin-yang*. The balance between fire and water in the body is crucial. Fire is essential to all physiological processes: it represents the flame that keeps alive and stokes all metabolic processes. Fire, the physiological fire, assists the heart its function of housing the mind (*shen*); it provides the warmth necessary to the spleen to transform and transport; it stimulates the small intestine function of separation; it provides the heat necessary to the bladder and lower burner to transform and excrete fluids and it provides the heat necessary for the uterus to keep the blood moving. If the physiological fire declines, the mind will suffer with depression, the spleen cannot transform and transport, the small intestine cannot separate the fluids, the bladder and lower burner cannot excrete the fluids and there will be oedema, and the uterus turns cold, which may cause infertility. This physiological fire is called the fire of the gate of life (*mingmen*) and derives from the kidney.

Water has the function of moistening and cooling during all the body's physiological functions, to balance the warming action of the physiological fire. The origin of water is also from the kidney. Thus, the balance between fire and water is fundamental to all physiological processes of the body. Fire and water balance and keep a check on each other in every single physiological process. When fire gets out of hand and becomes excessive, it has a tendency to flow upwards; hence the manifestations will show on the top part of the body and head, with headaches, red eyes, red face or thirst. When water becomes excessive, it has a tendency to flow downwards causing oedema of the legs, excessive urination or incontinence.

Yin and *yang* are opposite but are also mutually dependent on each other. *Yin* and *yang* cannot exist in isolation, and this is very apparent when considering the body's physiology. All the physiological processes are a result of the opposition and interdependence of *yin* and *yang*. The functions of the internal organs in Chinese medicine show the interdependence of *yin* and *yang* very clearly.

The *yin* and *yang* organs are very different in their functions, but, at the same time, they depend on each other for the performance of these functions. The *yin* organs depend on the *yang* ones to produce *qi* and blood from the transformation of food. The *yang* organs depend on the *yin* ones for their nourishment deriving from blood and essence stored by the *yin* organs.

Vocabulary

metabolism *n.* 新陈代谢
intestine *n.* 肠
oedema *n.* （医）水肿
kidney *n.* 肾；肾脏
opposition *n.* 对立；对立的事物
moisten *v.* （使）变得潮湿，变得湿润
symptomatic *adj.* 作为症状的；（有）症状的；作为证候的
spleen *n.* 脾
bladder *n.* 膀胱
uterus *n.* 子宫
manifestation *n.* 显示；表明；表明
derive *v.* 从……衍生出；起源于；来自

Exercises

1. Global reading

Decide whether the following statements are true（T）or false（F）.

（1）All symptoms and signs, complicated as they are, in Chinese medicine can be reduced to be the attributes of *yin* or *yang*.

（2）It is a close relationship between the theory of the five elements and that of *yin* and *yang*.

(3) The balance between fire and water is basic to all physiological processes of the body.

(4) All the physiological processes are a result of the opposition and inter transformation of *yin* and *yang*.

(5) The *yin* and *yang* organs are similar in their functions.

2. Questions for discussion

(1) What are the functions of the "fire of the gate of life" in maintaining the vitality of metabolic processes?

(2) What would happen to the physiological processes if balance between fire and water is disturbed?

(3) What are the functions of *yin* and *yang* organs that are mutually dependent on each other?

3. Classroom activities

(1) Wok in pairs and discuss How do you understand the theory of *yin* and *yang*?

(2) Can you give an example o illustrate the mutual consuming of *yin* and *yang* from a physiological point of view?

Text D
Yin and *Yang*: A Brief Introduction

In order to diagnose the nature of their patients' conditions practitioners need to understand and judge the relative balance of their *yin* and *yang qi*. One of the oldest classics of Chinese medicine, the Yellow Emperor's Classic of Internal Medicine (*Huangdi Neijing*) states:

To live in harmony with *yin* and *yang* means life.

To live against *yin* and *yang* means death.

To live in harmony with *yin* and *yang* will bring peace.

To live against *yin* and *yang* will bring chaos.

Yin and *yang* are now such commonly used terms that we could almost forget that they stem from the Chinese language. Used colloquially in English they describe opposite qualities. For example, light and dark, up and down, outside and inside and expansion and contraction are all qualities of *yin* and *yang*. However, opposite qualities are only partial descriptions of how *yin* and *yang* are used in the Chinese language.

Chinese medicine describes four main aspects of *yin* and *yang*. They are opposite to each other, dependent on each other, able to absorb or consume each other and able to transform into each other. Everything in the universe can be described as a combination of these two fundamental forces and they are in constant state of flux. *Yin* and *yang* gives recognition to the duality, interaction, interdependence and transformation of life.

Light and darkness are good examples to illustrate this. Light and darkness are opposite terms but they are also dependent on each other without darkness there would be no light; without light there would be no darkness.

We all have a different balance of *yin* and *yang*. Another way of understanding what these terms mean is to think of *yang* as fire; in other words, it is dry, bright, hot, active and moving upwards and outwards. *Yin*, on the other hand, is water as in a deep lake; it is wet, deep, dark, cold and still.

Just as the universe has its own dynamic balance of *yin* and *yang*, so, correspondingly does each individual. Chinese medicine tells us that in order to remain healthy we need live in harmony with *yin* and *yang* in our daily lives.

We all have a different balance of *yin* and *yang*. Another way of understanding what these terms mean is to think of *yang* as fire; in other words, it is dry, bright, hot, active and moving upwards and outwards. *Yin*, on the other hand, is water as in a deep lake; it is wet, deep, dark, cold and still.

Vocabulary

stem *n.* 起源于；根源是
colloquial *adj.*（词语和语言）口语；口语体；俗语
flux *n.* 不断地变动；不停地变化
consume *v.* 用尽，消耗，花费（某事物）
duality *n.* 两部分，双重
dynamic *adj.* 动力的
outward *adj.* 外面的；在外表的

Exercises

1. Global reading

Decide whether the following statements are true（T）or false（F）.

（1）*Yin* and *yang* are now such commonly used terms that we could almost forget that they stem from the Chinese language.

(2) Light and dark, up and down, outside and inside and expansion and contraction are all qualities of *qi*.

(3) Four aspects of *yin* and *yang* are opposite to each other, dependent on each other.

(4) In order to remain peace, we need live in harmony with *yin* and *yang* in our daily lives.

(5) We all have a different balance of *yin* and *yang*.

2. Questions for discussion

(1) What are the examples given in the text to describe *yin* and *yang* as opposite qualities?

(2) What are the four aspects of *yin* and *yang*?

(3) How to understand the balance of *yin* and *yang*.

Suggestion for Further Reading

Jeffery L. Greenwald. *Writing a History and Physical.* U. S. A: Elsevier Pte Ltd, 2006.

Unit 8 Chinese Festivals

The customs and fashions of men change like leaves on the bough, some of which go and others come.

——Dante

Unit Goals

- To learn to describe some customs of traditional Chinese festivals.
- To establish cultural awareness of traditional Chinese festivals.
- To learn the background of the origin of traditional Chinese festivals.
- To learn useful words and expressions that relates to traditional Chinese festivals and improve English languages skills.

Before You Read

1. Describe the customs of the following festivals according to the pictures.

2. Tell the origin of each festivals according to the pictures.

Intensive Reading

Text A
The Qing Ming Festival

《清明》

(唐) 杜牧

A drizzling rain falls like tears on the Mourning Day;
The mourner's heart is going to break on his way.
Where can a wineshop be found to drown his sad hours?
A cowherd points to a cot 'mid apricot flowers.

(许渊冲 译)

The Qing Ming Festival is the fifth one of the 24 traditional Chinese solar terms, falling on April 4–6 each year. Tomb Sweeping Day and the Clear Bright Festival are other common English translations of the Qing Ming Festival. After the festival, Temperatures begin to rise and rainfall increases, making it a crucial time for plowing and sowing in the spring. As trees turn green, flowers blossom, and the sun shines brightly, everything returns to life. It is a fine time to appreciate the beauty of nature.

This custom can be traced back to the Spring and Autumn Period (770–476 BC) and Warring States Period (475–221 BC). There is a person, who lived in Shanxi province in 600 BC legend has it that Jie saved his starving Lord's life by serving a piece of his own leg. When the Lord succeed in becoming the ruler of a small principality, he invited his faithful follower to join him. However, Jie declined his invitation, preferring to lead a hermit's life with his mother in the mountains. Believing that he could force Jie out by burning the mountain, the Lord ordered Jie men to set the forest on fire. To his consternation, Jie chose to remain where he was and was burnt to death. To commemorate Jie, the Lord ordered all fires in every home to be put out on the anniversary of Jie's death. Thus begun the "cold food feast", a day when no food could be cooked since no fire could be lit.

The "cold food" festival occurs on the eve of Qing Ming and is considered as part of the Qing Ming festival. As time passes, the Qing Ming festival replaced the "cold food" festival. And The Qingming Festival becomes an custom to remember and honor their ancestors at grave sites. Cleaning the tombs and paying respect to the dead with offerings are the two important practices to remember late relatives. Weeds around the tomb are cleared away and fresh soil is added to show care for the dead. The dead person's favorite food, wine and chopsticks are offered on their tombs, along with paper money. The rites have a long tradition in Asia, especially among farmers. Some people carry willow branches with them on Qing Ming, or put willow branches on their gates. They believe that willow branches help ward off the evil spirit that wanders on Qing Ming.

Legend has it that the Yellow Emperor first invented it for training warriors. Later, *Cu Ju* was used by people to build up their bodies when they were unable to eat hot food during the Cold Food Festival. People in the Jiangnan (south of the Yangtze River) region often eat this kind of green colored balls made from glutinous rice on Tomb Sweeping Day. The green color is from the juice of brome grass that is added in the rice.

Vocabulary

plow *n&v.* 犁，耕
sow *v.* 播（种子）；在（田地）里播种
principality *n.* 由王公贵族统治的小国；公国；侯国
consternation *n.* 惊恐；惊愕；惊慌
commemorate *v.* 纪念（伟人、大事件等）
anniversary *n.* 周年纪念日；周年纪念
willow *n.* 柳；柳树
glutinous *adj.* 似面筋的；黏的

After You Read

Exercises

1. Answer the following questions.

(1) When is the Qing Ming Festivals?
(2) Why do people celebrate the Qing Ming Festivals?
(3) What are the traditions of the Qing Ming Festivals?
(4) What traditional food do people usually eat on the Qing Ming Festivals?
(5) What customs are the Qing Ming Festivals?

2. Fill in the blanks with the words given below. Change the form where necessary. Each word can be used only once.

plow	commemorate	principality	sow	consternation
anniversary	blossom	ancestor	starve	glutinous

(1) The sauce was ____________ and tasted artificial.
(2) We ____________ the founding of our nation with a public holiday.
(3) The meadow has been ____________ up.
(4) A textbook which teaches the basic ____________ of geometry.
(5) A serious of movies will be shown to commemorate the 30th ____________ of his death.
(6) To her ____________, he asked her to make a speech.
(7) At this time of the year farmer ____________ their field.
(8) The cherry ____________ came out early in Washington this year.
(9) Her Chinese friends referred to the Empress as venerable ____________.
(10) The animals were left to ____________ to death.

3. Decide whether the statements are true (T) or false (F) according to the passage.

(1) After the festival, Temperatures and rainfall begin to rise, making it a crucial time for plowing and sowing in the spring.
(2) The "cold food" festival occurs on the same day of Qing Ming.
(3) Cleaning the tombs and paying respect to the dead with offerings are the two important practices to remember late relatives.
(4) Some people carry willow branches with them on Qing Ming in Asia.
(5) People in the north region often eat green colored balls made from glutinous rice on Tomb Sweeping Day.

4. Translation

(1) As trees turn green, flowers blossom, and the sun shines brightly, everything returns to life. It is a fine time to appreciate the beauty of nature.
(2) To commemorate Jie, the Lord ordered all fires in every home to be put out on the anniversary of Jie's death.
(3) Weeds around the tomb are cleared away and fresh soil is added to show care for the dead.

(4) And The Qing Ming Festival becomes an custom to remember and honor their ancestors at grave sites.

(5) Later, *Cu Ju* was used by people to build up their bodies when they were unable to eat hot food during the Cold Food Festival.

5. Pair work

Read the poem *The Qing Ming Festivals* with your partner loudly, Search a lot about The Qing Ming Festivals.

Read More
Extensive Reading

Text B
The Lantern Festival

The 15th day of the 1st lunar month is The Chinese Lantern Festival because the first lunar month is called Yuan-month and in the ancient times people called night Xiao. The 15th day is the first night to see a full moon. So the day is also called Yuan Xiao Festival in China. According to the Chinese tradition, at the very beginning of Yuan Xiao Festival, when there is a bright full moon hanging in the sky, there should be thousands of colorful lanterns hung out for people to appreciate.

In the history, Until the Song Dynasty in the sixth century, Emperor Yangdi invited guests from other countries to China to see the colorful lighted lanterns and enjoy the gala performances. By the beginning of the Tang Dynasty in the 7th century, the lantern displays would last three days. The emperor also lifted the curfew, allowing the people to enjoy the festive lanterns day and night , in some Chinese poems which describe this happy scene. In the Song Dynasty, The festival was celebrated for five days and the activities began to spread to many of the big cities in China. Colorful glass and even jade were used to make lanterns. With figures from folk tales Made on the lanterns. However, the largest Lantern Festival celebration took place in the early pert of the 15th century, The festivities continued for ten days. Emperor Chengzu had the downtown area set value as a center tor displaying the lanterns. Even today, there is a place in Beijing called Dengshikou. In Chinese, Deng means lantern and market, The area became a market where lanterns were sold during the day. In the evening, The local people would go there to see the beautiful lighted lanterns on display.

Riddles written on the lanterns can inspire wisdom and cater to the festival atmosphere, so many people like it very much. Guessing the answers to lantern riddles gradually became an indispensable part of the Lantern Festival.

Eating Yuan Xiao is another Lantern Festival tradition. Yuan Xiao is made of glutinous rice, either solid or stuffed. The stuffing includes bean paste, sugar, hawthorn, various kinds of fruit and so on. It can be boiled, fried or steamed and fried.

So it is a tradition that people hang lanterns everywhere, in their house or in the streets. The lanterns depict various characters, like flying birds, leaping fishes, and shining fireworks, showing an atmosphere of joy. People will come out and appreciate the beautiful scene.

In ancient times, young women, especially daughters of eminent families, hardly stepped out their houses. But during the Lantern Festival, it was a tradition that all people, including those young women, come out for lantern shows. Watching lanterns at night was just an opportunity for young women to find a man whose appearance appealed to them. Another activity, guessing the answers to lantern riddles, gives young people a chance to interact with each other and know more about each other. For thousands of years, there have been numerous love stories originating during the Lantern Festival.

Today, the displaying of lanterns is still a big event on the 15th day of the first lunar month throughout China. The People enjoy the brightly at night, Chengdu in Southwest China's Sichuan Province, For example, hold a lantern fair each year in the Cultural Park. The park is literally an ocean of lanterns. Many new designs attract countless visitors. The most eye-catching lantern is the Dragon Pole. This is a lantern in the shape of a golden Dragon. Spiraling up a 27meter high pole, spewing fireworks from its mouth. It is quite an impressive sight!

Vocabulary

curfew *n.* 宵禁

riddle *n.* 谜；谜语

glutinous *adj.* 似面筋的；黏的

spiral *adj.* 螺旋形的；盘旋的

gala *n.* （社交、体育、喜剧等的）特别场合，盛会

jade *n.* 玉，翡翠

indispensable *adj.* 不可缺少的；必需的

eminent *adj* 著名的，杰出的，卓越的

spew *v.* （使某事物）喷出，射出

Exercises

1. Global reading

Decide whether the following statements are true (T) or false (F).

(1) By the beginning of the Song Dynasty in the seventh century, the lantern displays would last three days.

(2) The festival was celebrated for five days and the activities began to spread to many of the big cities in China in the Song Dynasty.

(3) Now watching lanterns at night was just an opportunity for young women to find a man whose appearance appealed to them.

(4) For thousands of years, there have been numerous love stories originating during the Lantern Festival.

(5) Today, the exhibiting of lanterns is no longer a big event on the 15th day of the first lunar month throughout China.

2. Questions for discussion

(1) What are the Chinese traditions at the very beginning of Yuan Xiao Festival?

(2) How many days the largest Lantern Festival celebration?

(3) What Characters do lanterns can depict?

(4) What activities do they have for the young people in ancient times during the Lantern Festival?

(5) What activities do we have during the Lantern Festival?

3. Classroom activities

(1) Which activity has left the deepest impression on you in the Lantern Festivals? Please share with your classmates.

(2) Share your understandings about The Lantern Festivals gala with your classmates.

Text C
The Mid-Autumn Festival

The Mid-Autumn Festival is the second grandest festival after the Spring Festival in China. It takes its name from the fact that it is always celebrated in the middle of the autumn, On the day of the Mid-Autumn Festival, the moon is extremely bright and round. It's a time when families come together to appreciate the full moon and eat moon cakes during the festival. In fact, besides these two traditions, there are many others.

Worshiping the moon

Since ancient times, there has been a tradition of worshiping the moon in Mid-Autumn Festival in China, which stems from the deification of the moon by the ancients. On that day, people put the "god of the moon" sign, peaches, watermelons, moon cakes and other offerings on a table at home or outdoors, and then knelt down and kowtowed one by one, praying for blessings from the "god of the moon". Nowadays, this tradition is disappearing. It's rare to see families worshiping the moon in big cities. In some old towns or tourist cities, people will hold a ceremony to worship the moon in a square, park, or street, but this is more like a performance.

Watching the tide

In ancient times, watching the tide on the Qiantang River in East China's Zhejiang province was another grand event of Mid-Autumn Festival. The tide is very torrential and magnificent and attracts many onlookers. It had been recorded in detail since the Han Dynasty (206 BC–220). Many famous ancient poets, like Su Shi in the Song Dynasty (960–1279), wrote about the grand occasion in their poems. Today, watching the tide on the Qiantang River is still a characteristic event for the festival.

Making colorful lanterns

On the night of the Mid-Autumn Festival, the sky is clear as water, and the moon is full and bright like a mirror. People usually make colorful lanterns to decorate the beautiful night. They make the lanterns in different shapes to be hung on trees or houses, or floated on rivers. Park personnel will hang up colorful lanterns, which provide a beautiful scene at night. They also make *Kongming* lanterns, which can fly because the burning candles heat the air in the lantern. Children write good wishes on the lanterns and let them fly up into the sky.

Burning pagodas

In some places, burning pagodas during the Mid-Autumn Festival is another tradition. When night falls, people gather together in an empty place, and pick up broken bricks and tiles to pile up several pagodas, large and small. The pagodas are hollow and are stuffed with firewood. When all the pagodas are built up, someone will shout, "Ignite the fire!" Then, the firewood in the pagodas is lit, and the red flames rise and sparks explode, through which people express the joy of harvest in autumn.

Playing clay rabbit

The clay rabbit is a traditional handicraft in Beijing at Mid-Autumn Festival. Based on an image of the Jade Rabbit from the story of Chang'e in the Moon Palace, a clay rabbit is personalized and made in an artistic form. Some people imitate opera characters and carve the rabbit in a stylized way, such as a warrior with a golden helmet and armor, riding lions, elephants and other beasts of prey, or some riding peacocks, cranes and other birds. The rabbit figure once was an offering to worship the moon, but later, it became a popular children's toy.

Stealing vegetables

Among the Dong ethnic group in Central China's Hunan province, it is the custom for young ladies to steal vegetables on Mid-Autumn Festival night. There is a legend that during the Mid-Autumn Festival, the fairy in the Moon Palace will go down to the human world to spread sweet dew on the vegetables. Whoever eats vegetables with sweet dew on this night will be healthy and happy. Also, women and girls express their adoration to their favorite young men by this way.

Eating river snails

People believe that eating river snails in the Mid-Autumn Festival can make the eyes clear. River snails are rich in vitamin A, which is an important substance in visual pigments. Around the festival, there are no small river snails in the abdomens of larger river snails. Therefore, their meat is especially fat and delicious. It is the best time to eat river snails. Nowadays, many families in Guangzhou eat fried river snails during the festival.

Drinking osmanthus-flavored wine

Osmanthus flowers open and spread a sweet scent in autumn. Osmanthus-flavored wine is a gift during this season. Osmanthus fragrance is a symbol of prosperity and auspiciousness. Drinking osmanthus fragrance wine at Mid-Autumn Festival implies sweetness, wealth and auspiciousness, and prosperity of the family.

People gather together to appreciate the moon in which Wu Gang, is cutting a sweet-scented osmanthus tree outside the Moon Palace, according to a legend. They drink the sweet osmanthus-flavored wine to echo the festival atmosphere. Nowadays, some traditional customs are disappearing, and the younger generation have their own ways to spend the Mid-Autumn Festival, such as shopping, going to a party, or traveling, seemingly forgetting the traditional customs of the festival. This is because many in the post-80s and 90s generations are working and studying in other cities and some of them have many pressures in life. However, if they had chance, they would come back home to have a reunion dinner with their families.

Vocabulary

helmet *n.* 头盔
pigments *n.* 颜料
deification *n.* 神化
pagoda *n.* （印度和东亚的）塔，宝塔
ignite *v*（使某物）燃烧，着火；点火；点燃
kowtow *v.*（向某人或某事物）叩头，磕头，臣服
dew *n.* 露水
abdomen *n.* 腹部
torrential *adj.* 似急流的

Exercises

1. Global reading

Decide whether the following statements are true（T）or false（F）.

(1) It's common to see families worshiping the moon in big cities.
(2) Many famous ancient poets, like Su Shi in the Song Dynasty (960–1279), wrote about the grand occasion in their poems.
(3) Women and girls express their adoration to their favorite young men by Stealing vegetables.
(4) People believe that eating river snails in the Mid-Autumn Festival can make them healthy.
(5) Many young people still like drinking the sweet osmanthus-flavored wine to echo the festival atmosphere.

2. Questions for discussion

(1) What are the traditions on the day of the Mid-Autumn Festival?
(2) How did the people worship the moon in ancient times?
(3) What is the purpose of burning pagodas during the Mid-Autumn Festival?
(4) Why do people like eating river snails in the Mid-Autumn Festival?
(5) What do the Osmanthus fragrance symbolize?

3. Classroom activities

(1) How do your family celebrate tradition Mid-Autumn Festival? Is it different from

the customs described in the text?

(2) Share your understandings about the Mid-autumn Festival with your classmates.

Text D
Dragon Boat Festival

The Dragon Boat Festival, the 5th day of the 5th month in the Chinese lunar calendar, has had a history of more than 2,000 years. It is usually in June in the Solar calendar. Today, Dragon Boat Festival in the Chinese people is still a very popular grand festival. Country attaches great importance to the protection of intangible cultural heritage, On May 20, 2006, the State Council approved the inclusion of the folk first batch of national intangible cultural heritage.

Legends about Dragon Boat Festival

Qu Yuan was a famous poet during the Warring States period of Zhou Dynasty. He lived in Ancient State of Chu, which is Hubei province right now. The King of Chu decided to ally with Ancient State of Qin. Qu was banished for opposing this alliance and even accused of treason. During his exile, Qu Yuan wrote a great deal of poetry, including the famous *Li Sao* after Qu's exile, Qin invaded Chu. With despair, Qu Yuan committed suicide by drowning himself in the Miluo River. Local people raced out in their boats to save him or at least find his body. This is said to be the origin of Dragon Boat Race. When Qu Yuan's body couldn't be found, people dropped balls of sticky rice into the river, so that fish could heave enough to eat instead of Qu Yuan's body. This is said to be the origin of rice dumpling.

Customs about Dragon Boat Festival

Eating *Zongzi*

The most important traditional food for the Dragon Boat Festival is *zongzi*——pyramid shaped glutinous rice dumplings wrapped in reed leaves. According to legend, Jingchu people on May 5 to cook glutinous rice or steamed rice cake into the river to sacrifice Qu Yuan. Worried about being eaten by fish, they put glutinous rice into a bamboo tube and threw it into the river. Bamboo tube was gradually replaced by *Zongye* rice. In general, northern Chinese prefer sweet rice dumplings filled with red-bean paste or Chinese dates, while southerners like savory ones with fillings such as egg yolk, pork and mushroom.

Dragon Boat Racing

Dragon boat racing, a traditional Chinese sport originally held to celebrate the Dragon

Boat Festival, has gained global popularity and helped promote exchanges among countries. Unlike the evil or demonic creatures in European mythology, Asian dragons are traditionally believed to bring good fortune and prosperity.

Eating Salted Duck Eggs

Tradition has it that it is good to eat salted duck eggs during the Dragon Boat Festival as the burning summer is coming. The salted duck eggs are nutrient-rich and have some effect on the treatment of heatstroke.

***Jiandui*-Fried Cake**

Jiandui is a kind of fried round cake made of wheat and rice flour and something to sweeten them. In East China's Fujian province, every family eats *jiandui* on Dragon Boat Festival. A legend explains this custom. It is said that the area enters its rainy season during Dragon Boat Festival. People believed there were holes in the sky which, if not filled, would allow the rain to continue indefinitely. Eating *jiandui* is said to help mend the sky and fill the holes.

Mianshanzi

Mianshanzi is a kind of wheat flour food made in a fan shape. The custom of eating *mianshanzi* on the Dragon Boat Festival mainly prevails in Minqin county in Northwest China's Gansu province. This fan-shaped food is made up of five multi-colored layers, with each layer covered with fried sprinkles of pepper powder. The layers are pinched into a variety of patterns to make it appealing to eyes. This dietary custom is said to trace back to the tradition of making and selling fans during Duanwu Festival in ancient times.

Vocabulary

intangible *adj.* 难以形容（或理解）的；不易度量的；无形的（指没有实体存在的资本性资产）*n.* <商>（指企业资产）无形的

inclusion *n.* （被）包括，包含；被包括的人（或事物）

banish *v.* 放逐；流放；把（某人）驱逐出境；赶走；驱除

alliance *n.* （国家、政党等的）结盟，同盟；结盟团体；联盟

treason *n.* 危害国家罪，叛国罪（如战时通敌）

exile *n.* 流放；流亡；放逐；流亡国外者；被流放者；离乡背井者；*v.* 流放；放逐

heave *v.* （用力）举起，拖，拉，抛；（强烈而有节奏地）起伏；（常指吃力地）缓慢发出（声音）；*n.* 举；拖；拉；抛；起伏

savory *adj.* 令人愉快的；体面的；名声好的；好吃的；*n.* （饭前或饭后有助胃纳的）美味小盘菜肴；香草

demonic *adj.* 恶魔的；魔鬼似的；恶魔般的
heatstroke *n.* 中暑
prevail *v.* 普遍存在；盛行；流行；被接受；战胜；压倒；（尤指长时间斗争后）战胜，挫败
sprinkle *v.* 撒；洒；把…撒（或洒）在……上；使某物包含少量的另一物；用……点缀；下小雨；*n.* 小雨
pinch *v.* 拧；捏；掐；捏住；夹紧；夹（脚）；夹痛；*n.* 捏；掐；拧；一撮

Exercises

1. Global reading

Decide whether the following statements are true（T）or false（F）.

（1）On May 20, 2006, the State Council approved the inclusion of the folk first batch of national intangible cultural heritage.
（2）Qu Yuan wrote *Li Sao* during his exile because Qin invaded Chu.
（3）People cook glutinous rice or steamed rice cake into the river to commemorate Qu Yuan.
（4）Eating salted duck eggs has gained global popularity and helped promote exchanges among countries.
（5）The custom of eating *mianshanzi* on the Dragon Boat Festival mainly prevails in Minqin county in northwest China's Hubei province.

2. Questions for discussion

（1）What are the traditions on the day of the Dragon Boat Festival?
（2）Why did Qu Yuan commit suicide by drowning himself in the Miluo River?
（3）According to the passage, what is the difference between northerners and southerners when they eat *Zongzi*?
（4）Why did people eat *Jiandui* on the day of the Dragon Boat Festival?
（5）What is the feature of *Mianshanzi*?

3. Classroom activities

How do your family celebrate tradition of the Dragon Boat Festival? Is it different from the customs described in the text?
Share your understandings about the the Dragon Boat Festival with your classmates.

Key to Exercises

Unit 1　Chinese Philosophy

Text A

1. Answer the following questions.

   省略

2. Fill in the blanks with the words given below. Change the form where necessary. Each word can be used only once.

   (1) popularize　(2) inevitable　(3) unification　(4) divination

   (5) manipulating　(6) authorities　(7) contention　(8) incorporated

   (9) denounce　(10) Integrated

3. Decide whether the statements are true (T) or false (F) according to the passage.

   (1) T　(2) F　(3) F　(4) F　(5) F

4. Translation

   (1) 众所周知，商朝（公元前1600年–前1046年）早期的哲学思想是建立在循环论的基础上的，即通过观察昼夜循环、季节更替、月亮圆缺变化得来，这一概念与后来的中国哲学密切相关，并与偏线性的西方哲学方法区分开来。

   (2) 在接下来的周朝（公元前1122年–前256年），天命的概念被引入，天命认为上天会保佑公正统治者的权威，但不满于不明智的统治者，并收回天命。

   (3)《易经》描述了中国古代文化信仰所固有的古代宇宙观和哲学体系，其核心思想是对立的动态平衡、事件的演变过程和对变化必然性的接纳。

   (4) 在大约公元前500年，中国哲学的经典时期，百家争鸣，盛极一时，最具影响力的四个学派（儒家、道家、墨家和法家）确立下来。

   (5) 公元前221年，中国统一后的秦朝（也称帝王时代），法家学说取代墨家和儒家学派逐渐兴盛起来，尽管汉朝（公元前206年–公元220年）先后将道家和儒家学说确立为官方学说。

5. Pair work

省略

Text B

1. Global reading

Decide whether the following statements are true (T) or false (F).

(1) T　(2) F　(3) T　(4) T　(5) F

2. Questions for discussion

省略

3. Classroom activities

省略

Text C

1. Global reading

Decide whether the following statements are true (T) or false (F).

(1) F　(2) F　(3) F　(4) T　(5) F

2. Questions for discussion

省略

3. Classroom activities

省略

Text D

1. Global reading

Decide whether the following statements are true (T) or false (F).

(1) F　(2) F　(3) T　(4) F　(5) F

2. Questions for discussion

省略

3. Classroom activities

省略

Unit 2　Chinese Food

Text A

1. Answer the following questions.
   (1) One popular summary of Chinese food is "sweet in the south, salty in the north, sour in the west and spicy in the east."
   (2) Shandong cuisine, clear, pure and not greasy, is characterized by its emphasis on aroma, freshness, crispness and tenderness.
   (3) Chili. pepper , prickly ash, garlic, ginger and fermented soybean.
   (4) Jiangsu cuisine is well known for its careful selection of ingredients, its meticulous preparation methodology, and its not-too-spicy, not-too-bland taste.
   (5) Many kinds of porridges and refreshments provide enough nutrients to make up for the water lost through perspiration during the long, hot summer.
2. Fill in the blanks with the words given below. Change the form where necessary. Each word can be used only once.
   (1) designation　(2) adept　(3) enhance　(4) domestic
   (5) akin　(6) cuisine　(7) apt　(8) respective
   (9) aroma　(10) prevalent
3. Decide whether the statements are true (T) or false (F) according to the passage.
   (1) T　(2) F　(3) F　(4) T　(5) F
4. Translation
   (1) 济南菜系擅长炸、烤、煎、炒，而胶东菜系则以其烹饪海鲜的鲜淡而闻名。
   (2) 野菜和野禽常被选用为原料，油炸、无油炸、腌制和文火炖煮是基本的烹饪技术。
   (3) 浙江菜系由杭州菜、宁波菜、绍兴菜组成，不油腻，以其菜肴的鲜、柔、滑、香而闻名。
   (4) 闽菜经历了中原汉族文化和当地古越族文化的混合、交流而逐渐形成。
   (5) 安徽菜，又称徽菜，其独特之处不仅在于对烹饪食材的精挑细选，还在于其对烹饪过程的严格控制。
5. Pair work
   省略

Text B

1. Global reading

Decide whether the following statements are true (T) or false (F).

(1) T (2) F (3) F (4) F (5) T

2. Questions for discussion

省略

3. Classroom activities

省略

Text C

1. Global reading

Decide whether the following statements are true (T) or false (F).

(1) T (2) T (3) F (4) T (5) F

2. Questions for discussion

省略

3. Classroom activities

省略

Text D

1. Global reading

Decide whether the following statements are true (T) or false (F).

(1) F (2) T (3) F (4) T (5) F

2. Questions for discussion

省略

3. Classroom activities

省略

Unit 3 Chinese Tea

Text A

1. Answer the following questions.

省略

2. Fill in the blanks with the words given below. Change the form where necessary. Each word can be used only once.

   (1) calligraphy (2) original (3) due to (4) mellow
   (5) herbal (6) seep (7) host (8) essential
   (9) accompany (10) specialty

3. Decide whether the statements are true (T) or false (F) according to the passage.

   (1) T (2) F (3) T (4) F (5) T

4. Translation

   (1) 和中国功夫以及中药共同作为一种生动的中国文化特色，茶在中国发展了很长一段时间，形成了一系列的茶文化。
   (2)《茶经》代表了中国茶不仅在饮食中占有重要地位，而且茶文化也渗透到人们日常生活的各个方面，如诗歌、绘画、书法、宗教、医药等。
   (3) 茶叶浸泡一两次后通常被丢弃。
   (4) 在今天的中国，茶仍然在人们的日常生活中扮演着重要的角色，尤其是在家里、餐馆和茶馆。
   (5) 如今，在中国很多关于茶的知识仍然被视为无价的遗产，茶仍然是餐桌上常见的饮料，甚至成为人们招待或拜访他人的理想礼物。

5. Pair work

   省略

Text B

1. Global reading

   Decide whether the following statements are true (T) or false (F).

   (1) T (2) F (3) T (4) F (5) T

2. Questions for discussion

   省略

3. Classroom activities

   省略

Text C

1. Global reading

   Decide whether the following statements are true (T) or false (F).

   (1) T (2) F (3) T (4) F (5) T

2. Questions for discussion

省略

3. Classroom activities

省略

Text D

1. Global reading

Decide whether the following statements are true (T) or false (F).

(1) T　(2) F　(3) F　(4) T　(5) T

2. Questions for discussion

省略

3. Classroom activities

省略

Unit 4　Chinese Traditional Architecture

Text A

1. Answer the following questions.

省略

2. Fill in the blanks with the words given below. Change the form where necessary. Each word can be used only once.

(1) anthology　(2) architecture　(3) decorative　(4) vermilion
(5) heightened　(6) harmony　(7) increasing　(8) artist
(9) monotonous　(10) sculpture

3. Decide whether the statements are true (T) or false (F) according to the passage.

(1) F　(2) T　(3) T　(4) F　(5) T

4. Translation

(1) 中国建筑是一种建筑风格，在东亚已经形成了几个世纪。

(2) 中国古人充分利用了屋顶的特点。

(3) 在中国古代的宫殿或寺庙中，用背景建筑来表现艺术和美感是很常见的。

(4) 中国古代的工匠有用色的勇气，善于用色，这与中国建筑的木结构体系有着密切的联系。

(5) 中国建筑师在长期的实践中积累了丰富的色彩运用经验。

5. 省略

Text B

1. Global reading

   Decide whether the following statements are true (T) or false (F).

   (1) T (2) F (3) T (4) T (5) T

2. Questions for discussion

   省略

3. Classroom activities

   省略

Text C

1. Global reading

   Decide whether the following statements are true (T) or false (F).

   (1) T (2) F (3) F (4) T (5) T

2. Questions for discussion

   省略

3. Classroom activities

   省略

Text D

1. Global reading

   Decide whether the following statements are true (T) or false (F).

   (1) T (2) T (3) F (4) F (5) F

2. Questions for discussion

   省略

3. Classroom activities

   省略

Unit 5 Chinese Literature

Text A

1. Answer the following questions.

(1) What all four have in common is that they were written in a spoken language of their times.

(2) It is historical fiction about the lives and struggles of rulers and the wars at the end of the Han Dynasty and in the Three Kingdoms Period.

(3) The setting of the novel is during the Northern Song Dynasty era before the northern part of the Song Empire was overrun by a northern tribe and before the Mongols conquered the whole area.

(4) Chang'an was near the mouth of the Gansu Corridor that was a part of the Silk Road route in northwestern China.

(5) 13 years.

2. Fill in the blanks with the words given below. Change the form where necessary. Each word can be used only once.

(1) Buddhism (2) intrigue (3) marsh (4) viciously

(5) machinations (6) outlaw (7) clans (8) vernaculars

(9) alliance (10) seminal

3. Decide whether the statements are true (T) or false (F) according to the passage.

(1) F (2) T (3) T (4) F (5) F

4. Translation

(1) 它是一部关于汉末三国时期统治者的生活、斗争和战争的历史小说。

(2) 小说的背景是北宋时期，宋朝北部被北方部落占领，蒙古人征服了整个地区。

(3) 他穿过甘肃走廊，经过吐鲁番附近的火焰山。

(4) 在唐朝，一个名叫玄奘的佛教徒离开了长安（今西安），那里是唐朝的首都，他到印度去收集经文和信息。

(5) 故事讲述清朝（1644-1991年）两个家族的命运和生活。

5. Pair work

省略

Text B

1. Global reading

Decide whether the following statements are true (T) or false (F).

(1) T (2) T (3) F (4) F (5) F

2. Questions for discussion

省略

3. Classroom activities

省略

Text C

1. Global reading

Decide whether the following statements are true (T) or false (F).

(1) T　　(2) T　　(3) F　　(4) T　　(5) T

2. Questions for discussion

省略

3. Classroom activities

省略

Text D

1. Global reading

Decide whether the following statements are true (T) or false (F).

(1) F　　(2) T　　(3) F　　(4) T　　(5) F

2. Questions for discussion

省略

3. Classroom activities

省略

Unit 6　Chinese Operas

Text A

1. Answer the following questions.

(1) Chinese opera together with Greece tragic-comedy and Indian Sanskrit Opera are the three oldest dramatic art forms in the world.

(2) During the Qing Dynasty (1644–1911), it became fashionable among ordinary people.

(3) It evolved from folk songs, dances, talking, antimasque, and especially distinctive dialectical music.

(4) Three main techniques: distinctive techniques of painting; lines also function as symbols; the marvelous acrobatics.

2. Fill in the blanks with the words given below. Change the form where necessary. Each word can be used only once.

(1) evolved (2) melody (3) trait (4) viperous
(5) fascinate (6) intangible (7) dramatic (8) squatted
(9) makeshift (10) heritage

3. Decide whether the following statements are true (T) or false (F).

(1) F (2) T (3) T (4) T (5) T

4. Translation

(1) 中国戏曲、希腊悲喜剧和印度梵语歌剧是世界上最古老的三种戏剧艺术形式。

(2) 自元朝（1271 - 1368 年）以来，它一直受到朝廷官员和皇帝的鼓励，并已成为一种传统的艺术形式。

(3) 演员们在二胡、铜锣、琵琶等传统乐器的伴奏下，演奏出独特的旋律，并附以优美的文笔和具有很高文学价值的对白，这对外国人来说可能听起来很奇怪。

(4) 表演者可以在表演时从口中喷出火焰，也可以在蹲着扮演矮人时飞奔。

(5) 在过去的 800 年里，中国戏曲根据地方特色和口音演变成许多不同的地方品种。

5. Pair work

省略

Text B

1. Global reading

Decide whether the following statements are true (T) or false (F).

(1) F (2) T (3) F (4) F (5) T

2. Questions for discussion

(1) There are more than 360 types of Chinese operas, with Beijing Opera, Huangmei Opera, Yue Opera and Yu Opera considered the four most famous.

(2) Because the Beijing Opera was originally a feature of the imperial palace, it had stricter requirements for the performance, costumes, makeup and songs.

(3) Legend says that because Huangmei is located on the northern bank of the Yangtze River, it was frequently struck by natural disasters, especially floods.

3. Classroom activities

省略

Text C

1. Global reading

Decide whether the following statements are true (T) or false (F).

(1) T (2) T (3) F (4) F (5) T

2. Questions for discussion

(1) There are four roles in Beijing Opera-*Sheng* (a male role, usually a leading one), *Dan* (female roles), *Jing* (painted-face roles) and *Chou* (Clown role).

(2) Opera facial painting falls into four categories-personality makeup (facial designs, painted faces or Lian Pu), decorative makeup (decorated faces), mood makeup (changing facial designs), and pictographic makeup (animal-like facial designs).

(3) Art of illusion and imagination is one of Beijing Opera's most important features, expressed through exaggeration and concentration.

A decorated whip represents horse, a paddle a boat and two pennants embroidered with wheels a carriage. When the actor walks in a circle, it means that he is in a long journey. Four generals and four soldiers represent an army. Two actors can portray groping and fighting dark through dance and acrobatics on a brightly lit stage.

3. Classroom activities

省略

Text D

1. Global reading

Decide whether the following statements are true (T) or false (F).

(1) F (2) T (3) T (4) F (5) T

2. Questions for discussion

(1) In 2001, UNESCO (United Nations Educational, Cultural and Scientific Organization) proclaimed Kunqu Opera as a masterpiece of the Oral and Intangible Heritage of humanity.

(2) Because it requires a high level of technical knowledge from the audience.

(3) The action plan aims to publish a complete edition of the texts of Kunqu Operas since the Ming era, to produce an archive of the expertise of elderly actors

through video recordings and to revive those plays which have not been performed for a considerable time.

3. Classroom activities

省略

Unit 7 Traditional Chinese Medicine

Text A

1. Answer the following questions.

省略

2. Fill in the blanks with the words given below. Change the form where necessary. Each word can be used only once.

(1) therapeutic (2) diagnosed (3) Physiology (4) Compilation
(5) Pathology (6) Syndrome (7) herb (8) Miscellaneous
(9) Clinical (10) Diagnostic

3. Decide whether the statements are true (T) or false (F) according to the passage.

(1) F (2) F (3) T (4) F (5) T

4. Translation

(1) 中医有着几千年的历史，它有着独特而完整的理论体系、丰富的经验和良好的效果，为中华民族的健康和中华民族的发展作出了巨大的贡献。
(2) 中医学理论体系事物形成可以追溯到战国和秦国时期。
(3)《难经》在许多方面，尤其在脉学长，补《黄帝内经》之不足。
(4)《黄帝内经》是中国现存最早的病因证候学专著。

5. Pair work

省略

Text B

1. Global reading

Decide whether the following statements are true (T) or false (F).

(1) F (2) F (3) T (4) T (5) F

2. Questions for discussion

省略

3. Classroom activities

省略

Text C

1. Global reading

   Decide whether the following statements are true (T) or false (F).

   (1) T (2) T (3) T (4) F (5) T

2. Questions for discussion

   省略

3. Classroom activities

   省略

Text D

1. Global reading

   Decide whether the following statements are true (T) or false (F).

   (1) T (2) F (3) T (4) F (5) F

2. Questions for discussion

   省略

Unit 8 Chinese Festivals

Text A

1. Answer the following questions.

   省略

2. Fill in the blanks with the words given below. Change the form where necessary. Each word can be used only once.

   (1) glutinous (2) commemorate (3) plowed (4) principal
   (5) anniversary (6) consternation (7) sow (8) blossom
   (9) ancestor (10) starve

3. Decide whether the statements are true (T) or false (F) according to the passage.

   (1) T (2) F (3) T (4) T (5) F

4. Translation

   (1) 树木变绿，鲜花盛开，阳光灿烂，一切都回归生活。这是欣赏自然之美的好时机。
   (2) 为了纪念杰，君王下令在杰死周年之际扑灭每个家庭的所有火灾。
   (3) 坟墓周围的杂草被清除，并添加新鲜的土壤，以显示对死者的缅怀。

(4) 清明节成为在坟地怀念先祖的习俗。

(5) 后来，当人们在寒食节期间不能吃热食时，蹴鞠被人们用来锻炼他们的身体。

5. Pair work

省略

Text B

1. Global reading

Decide whether the following statements are true (T) or false (F).

(1) F (2) T (3) F (4) T (5) F

2. Questions for discussion

省略

3. Classroom activities

省略

Text C

1. Global reading

Decide whether the following statements are true (T) or false (F).

(1) F (2) T (3) T (4) F (5) T

2. Questions for discussion

省略

3. Classroom activities

省略

Text D

1. Global reading

Decide whether the following statements are true (T) or false (F).

(1) T (2) F (3) T (4) F (5) F

2. Questions for discussion

省略

3. Classroom activities

省略